TEACHING CHILDREN
TO RELAX

ABOUT THE AUTHOR

James H. Humphrey, Professor Emeritus at the University of Maryland, has been a recognized authority on child development and learning for over three decades. A pioneer in stress education, he collaborated with the late Hans Selye — who is generally known as the "Father of Stress" — on certain aspects of childhood stress research. He is the author or coauthor of over 40 books which have been adopted for use in over 1200 colleges and universities. He has written 13 children's books and is the creator of four educational record albums. In addition, his 200 articles and research reports have appeared in over 20 different national and international journals.

TEACHING CHILDREN
TO RELAX

By

JAMES H. HUMPHREY, Ed.D.

Professor Emeritus
University of Maryland
College Park, Maryland

CHARLES C THOMAS • PUBLISHER
Springfield • Illinois • U.S.A.

Published and Distributed Throughout the World by
CHARLES C THOMAS • PUBLISHER
2600 South First Street
Springfield, Illinois 62794-9265

© *1988 by* CHARLES C THOMAS • PUBLISHER
ISBN 0-398-05512-2
Library of Congress Catalog Card Number: 88-16075

With THOMAS BOOKS *careful attention is given to all details of manufacturing
and design. It is the Publisher's desire to present books that are satisfactory as to their
physical qualities and artistic possibilities and appropriate for their particular use.*
THOMAS BOOKS *will be true to those laws of quality that assure a good name
and good will.*

Printed in the United States of America
Q-R-3

Library of Congress Cataloging in Publication Data
Humphrey, James Harry, 1911-
    Teaching children to relax/by James H. Humphrey.
      p. cm.
    Bibliography: p.
    Includes index.
    ISBN 0-398-05512-2
    1. Students—Mental health—United States. 2.
Classroom environment—United States. 3. Stress
(Psychology) 4. Relaxation.
I. Title.
LB3013.25.H85 1988
371.7′1—dc19   88-16075
                              CIP

PREFACE

A LITTLE over a year ago I was interviewed by a feature writer for a large metropolitan newspaper about my work in childhood stress. The resulting newsstory generated a great deal of positive feedback from educators, representatives of the U.S. Office of Education and assorted congressional committees. This interest focused mainly upon the stressfulness of the school day and the need to help relieve children of the stress and tension thereof with periodic relaxation programs. Thus, this book was conceived.

Since many of the psychological causes of tension begin early in life it is extremely important that attention be given to this during the early school years. No question about it, learning to relax as a child could be as important to life in the future as many other lessons learned in school. In fact, relaxation is a fundamental basic need in the same way as food, sleep and physical activity. Children need frequent periods of relaxation to carry on the daily school tasks required of them.

From an historical point of view, for many decades schools have scheduled "recess" as a means of mental diversion so that children can "refresh" themselves for the many mental tasks of the school day. However, this is not enough in our complex and complicated modern society. More sophisticated programs need to be incorporated as a part of the school day.

I am pleased to be able to report that this is now occurring in some remote instances, but it needs to be much more widespread than it is at the present time.

It is the express purpose of the content of this book to provide information for teachers and other educators to use to reach this objective. The first three chapters are intended to help the reader form a basic attitude and understanding of child development, childhood emotions and the extent of stress in the school environment.

Chapters 4 through 7 are devoted to a consideration of how deep muscle relaxation can be used by teachers and other educators and how they can use it with children. These chapters include discussions about the meaning and theory of relaxation, formal classroom relaxation exercises, relaxation games and stunts and relaxation through creative movement.

The last five chapters are more concerned with psychological aspects of relaxation and include discussions of mental practice and imagery, the quieting reflex, systematic desensitization, meditation and biofeedback.

All of the practices recommended throughout the book have been extensively field-tested with children and have been found to be successful when applied in the appropriate manner.

Although the book is intended for school personnel, others who deal with children in the out-of-school situation may also find the materials of practical use.

James H. Humphrey

CONTENTS

TEACHING CHILDREN
TO RELAX

Chapter 1

UNDERSTANDING
CHILD DEVELOPMENT

TEACHING children to relax should begin with a clear understanding of child development and childhood emotions — the subjects of this and the following chapter.

Development is concerned with changes in the child's ability to function at an increasingly higher level. For example, a stage of development in the infant is from creeping to crawling. This is later followed by the developmental stage of walking when the child moves to an upright position and begins to move over the surface area by putting one foot in front of the other.

There are several major theories of child development and each has its own devoted followers. The position taken here is that there are various aspects of each theory that are useful to those adults — parents, teachers and others — who have responsibilities for guiding children through the developmental years. It will be the purpose here, therefore, to make some generalizations of the various theories in an effort to provide useful information for adults to apply in their dealings with children.

Regardless of the theory or combinations of theories of child development that one believes in, all children are going to experience some sort of undesirable stress with the resulting need for relaxation at one time or another. Many children may never have to contend with more than the average amount of stress that is caused by the growth and developmental process. However, other children may be encumbered with such serious life stressors as divorce, hospitalization, death in the family and the like.

In general, it is believed that there are about three classifications of children in terms of their ability to deal with stress and tension. There is one group of children that seems to cope with stress extremely well.

They recover soon and are able to incorporate the stressful experience into their everyday life experiences. They have a great deal of confidence in themselves and when they encounter a stressful situation and cope with it successfully, their self-confidence tends to increase. Incidentally, these are the children who are associated with adults who deal well with stress.

Another group of children consists of those who can cope with stress to some extent, but they have to "work at it." They gain more self-confidence as they improve their ability to cope. However, they do not seem to have as high a level of successes as those classified as "exceptional copers."

The third level of classification involves those children who have a great deal of difficulty in coping with stress. They have problems struggling with some of the processes of normal growth and development. In addition, they become upset and disorganized by the daily hassles as well as life event stressors. As might be expected, this group of children associates with adults (particularly parents) who also have a difficult time adjusting to certain life situations that bring about stress.

The aim of adults, of course, should be to help all children become successful in their dealings with undersirable stress. With some knowledge of child development, teachers and others should be in a better position to provide environments that will help children cope effectively with stress and tension during their developmental years.

TOTAL DEVELOPMENT OF THE CHILD

There is a great deal of evidence that indicates that a human being must be considered as a whole and not a collection of parts. This means that a child is a unified individual, or what is more popularly known as the **whole** child. Teachers and others should think in terms of working in the direction of total development of children in order to adequately meet their developmental needs.

Total development consists of the sum of all the **physical, social, emotional** and **intellectual** aspects of any individual. Thus, these aspects become the various major **forms** of development. Of course, there are other forms of development, but they can be satisfactorily subclassified under the above major forms. For example, **motor** development, which is defined as a progressive change in motor performance, is considered as a broader part of the aspect of **physical** development. In addition, **moral** development, which is concerned with the capacity of the individual to distinguish between standards of right and wrong, could be considered as a dimension of the broad aspect of **social** development. This is to say that moral development involving achievement in ability to determine right from wrong is influential in the individual's social behavior.

Total development is "one thing" comprising the various major forms of development. All of these components — physical, social, emotional and intellectual — are highly interrelated and interdependent. All are of importance to well-being. The condition of any one of these forms of development affects other forms to a degree and, thus, total development as a whole. When a nervous child stutters or becomes nauseated, a mental state is not necessarily causing a physical symptom. On the contrary, a pressure imposed upon the child causes a series of reactions, which include thought, verbalization, digestive processes, and muscular function. It is not always necessarily true that the mind causes the body to become upset; the total organism is upset by a particular situation and reflects its upset in several ways, including disturbance in thought, feeling, and bodily processes. The whole child responds in interaction with the social and physical environment, and as the child is affected by the environment, he or she in turn has an effect upon it.

The foregoing statements have attempted to point out rather forcefully that the major forms of development are basic components that make for total development of the child. However, each of these forms of development have certain specific concerns and as such warrant separate discussions. This appears extremely important if one is to understand the place of each form of development as an integral part of total development. The following discussions of the physical, social, emotional and intellectual forms of development as they relate to children should be viewed in this general frame of reference.

Physical Development

One point of departure in discussing physical development could be to say that "everybody has a body." Some are short, some are tall, some are lean and some are fat. Children come in different sizes, but all of them are born with certain capacities that are influenced by the environment.

It might be said of the child that he "is" his body. It is something he can see. It is his base of operation. The other components of total development — social, emotional and intellectual — are somewhat vague as far as the child is concerned. Although these are manifested in various ways, children do not always see them as they do the physical aspect. Consequently, it becomes important that a child be helped early in life to gain some degree of control over his body, or what is known as **basic body control**. The ability to do this, of course, will vary from one child to another. It will likely depend upon the status of physical fitness of the child. The broad area of physical fitness can be broken down into certain components, and it is important that children achieve to the best of their ability with these components. Although there is not complete agreement on the identification of these components, the general consensus is that they consist of muscular strength, endurance and power, circulatory-respiratory endurance, agility, speed, flexibility, balance and coordination.

Social Development

Human beings are social beings. They work together for the benefit of society. They have fought together in time of national emergencies in order to preserve the kind of society they believe in, and they play together. While all this may be true, social development is still quite vague and confusing, particularly where children are concerned.

It was a relatively easy matter to identify certain components of physical fitness such as strength, endurance and the like. However, this does not necessarily hold true for components of social fitness. The components of physical fitness are the same for children as for adults. On the other hand, the components of social fitness for children may be different from the components of social fitness for adults. By some adult standards children might be considered as social misfits because certain behaviors of children might not be socially acceptable to some adults.

To the chagrin of some adults, especially parents, young children are uninhibited in their social development. In this regard we need to be concerned with social maturity as it pertains to the growing and ever-changing child. This is to say that we need to give consideration to certain characteristics of social maturity and how well they are dealt with at the different stages of child development. Perhaps teachers and others should ask themselves such questions as, Are we helping children to become more self-reliant by giving them independence at the proper time? Are we helping them to be outgoing and interested in others as well as themselves? Are we helping them to know how to satisfy their own needs in a socially desirable way? Are we helping them to develop a wholesome attitude toward themselves and others?

Emotional Development

In considering the subject of emotion, we are confronted with the fact that for many years it has been a difficult concept to define, and, in addition, there have been many changing ideas and theories in the study of emotion. A few general statements relative to the nature of emotion will appear here, and Chapter 2 will deal with childhood emotions in some detail.

Emotion could be defined as a response an individual makes when confronted with a situation for which he or she is unprepared or which is interpreted as a possible source of gain or loss. As will be seen in the following chapter, there are pleasant emotions and those that are unpleasant. For example, joy could be considered a pleasant emotional experience, while fear would be an unpleasant one. It is interesting to note that a good proportion of the literature is devoted to emotions that are unpleasant. It has been found that in books on psychology much more space is given to such emotional patterns as fear, hate and guilt than to such pleasant emotions as love, sympathy and contentment.

Generally speaking, the pleasantness or unpleasantness of an emotion seems to be determined by its strength or intensity, by the nature of the situation arousing it, and by the way a child perceives or interprets the situation. The emotions of young children tend to be more intense than those of adults. If adults are not aware of this aspect of child behavior, they will not be likely to understand why a child reacts rather violently to a situation that to them seems somewhat insignificant. The fact that different children will react differently to the same type of situation also should be taken into account. For example, something that might anger one child might have a rather passive influence on another.

Intellectual Development

Children possess varying degrees of intelligence, and most fall within a range of what is called "normal" intelligence. In dealing with this form of development, we should perhaps give attention to what might be considered as components of intellectual fitness. However, this is difficult to do. Because of the somehat vague nature of intelligence, it is practically impossible to identify specific components of it. Thus, we need to view intellectual fitness in a somewhat different manner.

For purposes of this discussion, intellectual fitness will be considered from a standpoint of how certain things influence intelligence. If we know this, then we might understand better how to contribute to intellectual fitness by improving upon some of these factors. Some of the factors that tend to influence intelligence are: (1) health and physical condition, (2) emotional disturbance, (3) certain social and economic factors, and (4) children under stress. When adults have a realization of these factors, perhaps they will be more able to deal satisfactorily with children in helping them in their intellectual pursuits.

STAGES OF DEVELOPMENT

In considering the various developmental stages of children, it should be understood that descriptions of such stages reflect the characteristics of the so-called "average" child. Although children are more alike than they are different, they all differ in a least one or more characteristics, even identical twins. Therefore, the reader is reminded that the general traits and characteristics included in the following discussion are suggestive of the behavior of the "normal" child. This implies that if a given child does not conform to these characteristics, it should not be interpreted to mean that he or she is seriously deviating from the norm. In other words, it should be recognized that each child progresses at his or her own rate and that there is likely to be overlapping from one stage of development to another.

The first stage of development is considered to be that period from birth to 15 months. This can be designated as the "intake" stage, because behavior and growth is characterized by **taking in.** This not only applies to food but to other things such as sound, light and the various forms of total care.

At this stage **separation anxiety** can occur. Since the child is entirely dependent upon the mother or other caregiver for needs being met, separation may be seen as being deprived of these important needs. It is at this stage that the child's overseer (ordinarily the parent) should try to maintain a proper balance between meeting the child's needs and "overgratification." Many child-development specialists seem to agree that children who experience some stress and tension from separation, or from having to wait for a need to be fulfilled, are gaining the opportunity to organize their psychological resources and adapt to stress. On the contrary, children who do not have this balance may be those who tend to disorganize under stress. They fall into the previously mentioned third level of classification of children who have a great deal of difficulty coping with stress.

During the stage from about 15 months to three years children are said to develop autonomy. This can be described as "I am what I can do" stage. Autonomy develops because most children can now move about rather easily. The child does not have to rely entirely on a caregiver to meet every single need. Autonomy also results from the development of mental processes, because the child can think about things and put language to use.

It is during this stage that the process of toilet training can be a major stressor. Children are not always given the needed opportunity to express autonomy during this process. It can be a difficult time for the child, because he is ordinarily expected to cooperate with and gain the approval of the principal caregiver. If the child cooperates and uses the toilet, approval is forthcoming; however, some autonomy is lost. If he does not cooperate, disapproval is likely to result. If this conflict is not resolved satisfactorily, some clinical psychologists believe it will emerge during adulthood in the form of highly anxious and compulsive behaviors.

The next stage, from three to five years, can be described as "I am what I think I am." Skills of body movement are being used in a more purposeful way. Children develop the ability to daydream and make believe and these are used to manifest some of their behaviors. Pretending allows them to be what they want to be — anything from animals to astronauts. It is possible, however, that resorting to fantasy may result in stress because they may become scared of their own such fantasies.

The range of age levels from five through seven years usually includes children from kindergarten through second grade. During this period the child begins his formal education. In our culture he leaves the home for a part of the day to take his place in a classroom with children of approximately the same age. Not only is he taking an important step toward becoming increasingly more independent and self-reliant, but as he learns he moves from being a highly self-centered individual to becoming a more socialized member of the group.

This stage is usually characterized by a certain lack of motor coordination, because the small muscles of the hands and fingers are not as well developed as the large muscles of the arms and legs. Thus, as he starts his formal education the child needs to use large crayons or pencils as one means of expressing himself. His urge to action is expressed through movement, since he lives in a movement world, so to speak. Children at these age levels thrive on vigorous activity. They develop as they climb, run, jump, hop, skip or keep time to music. An important physical aspect at this stage is that the eyeball is increasing in size and the eye muscles are developing. This factor is an important determinant in the child's readiness to see and read small print, and, thus, it involves a sequence from large print on charts to primer type in preprimers and primers.

Even though he has a relatively short attention span, he is extremely curious about the environment. At this stage, adults can capitalize upon the child's urge to learn by providing opportunities for him to gain information from firsthand experiences through the use of the senses. He sees, hears, smells, feels and even tastes in order to learn.

The age range from eight to nine years is the stage that usually marks the time spent in the third and fourth grade. The child now has a wider range of interests and a longer attention span. While strongly individualistic, the child is working more from a position in the group. Organized games should afford opportunities for developing and practicing skills in good leadership and followership as well as body control, strength and endurance. Small muscles are developing, manipulative skills are increasing and muscular coordination is improving. The eyes have developed to a point where the child can, and does, read more widely. The child is capable of getting information from books and is beginning to learn more through vicarious experience. However, experiments carry an impact for learning at this stage by capitalizing upon the child's curiosity. This is the stage of the child's development when skills of communication (listening, speaking, reading and writing) and the number system are needed to deal with situations both in and out of school.

During the ages of ten through twelve most children complete fifth and sixth grades. This is a period of transition for most as they go from childhood into the preadolescent period in their development. They may show concern over bodily changes and are sometimes self-conscious about appearance. At this stage children tend to differ widely in physical maturation and emotional stability. Greater deviations in development can be noted within sex groups than between them. Rate of physical growth can be rapid, sometimes showing itself in poor posture and restlessness. Some of the more highly organized team games such as softball, modified soccer and the like help furnish the keen and wholesome competition desired by children in this stage of development. It is essential that teachers and others recognize that, at this stage, prestige among peers is more important than adult approval. During this stage, the child is ready for a higher level of intellectual skills which involve reasoning, discerning fact from opinion, noting cause-and-effect relationships, drawing conclusions, and using various references to locate and compare the validity of information. The child is beginning to show more proficiency in expressing himself through oral and written communication.

Thus, after the child enters school and completes the elementary school years, he develops: (1) socially, from a self-centered individual to a participating member of a group; (2) emotionally, to a higher degree of self-control; (3) physically, from childhood to the brink of adolescence; and (4) intellectually, from learning by firsthand experiences to learning from more technical and specialized resources.

MEETING THE NEEDS OF CHILDREN

Many child psychologists believe that undesirable stress and tension may be due primarily to the failure of adults to help children meet their needs.

In discussing needs of children it is important to consider their **interests** as well. Although needs and interests of children are closely related and highly interdependent, there are certain important differences that need to be taken into account.

Needs of children, particularly those of an individual nature, are likely to be innate. On the other hand, interests may be acquired as products of the environment. It is possible that a child may demonstrate an interest in certain unsafe practice that is obviously not in accord with his needs at a certain age level. The two-year-old may be interested in running into the street, but this practice might result in injury. Acquiring a particular interest because of environmental conditions is further illustrated in the case of children coming from families that are superstitious about certain kinds of foods or certain foods eaten in combination. In such cases acquiring such an interest from other family members might build up a lifetime resistance to a certain kind of food that might be very nutritious and beneficial to the child's physical needs.

One of the most important aspects is that of obtaining a proper balance between needs and interests. However, arriving at a suitable ratio between needs and interests is not an easy task. Although we should undoubtedly think first in terms of meeting the child's needs, we must also have his interest. A general principle by which we might be guided is that the **lower** the age level of children, the more we should take the responsibility for meeting their needs. This is based on the obvious assumption that the younger the child, the less experience he has had, and consequently there is less opportunity to develop certain interests. In other words, a lack of interest at an early age level might possibly be synonymous with ignorance.

Classification of Needs

It is a well-known fact that children's needs have been classified in many ways. However, it should be borne in mind that any classification of needs is usually an arbitrary one made for a specific purpose. For example, when one speaks of biological needs and psychological needs it should be understood that each of these, although classified separately, are interdependent. The classification of needs used here is the same that was used for the forms of development. That is, physical, social, emotional and intellectual needs.

Physical Needs

Needs of a physical nature are concerned with the basic anatomical structure and basic physiological function of the human organism. Included here, of course, are the need for food, rest and activity, and proper care of the eyes, ears, teeth, and the like. Physical needs are also concerned with such factors as strength, endurance, agility, flexibility and balance that were previously considered as elements of physical fitness of the human organism. It is interesting to note that the physical aspect can be measured most accurately with objective instruments. We can tell how tall or heavy a child is at any stage of development. Moreover, persons trained for the purpose can derive accurate information with measurements of blood pressure, blood counts, urinalysis and the like.

Social Needs

The importance of social needs is brought more clearly into focus when we consider that most of what human beings do they do together. Social maturity, and hence social fitness, might well be expressed in terms of fulfillment of certain needs. In other words, if certain social needs are being adequately met, the child should be in a better position to realize social fitness. Among other needs, we must give consideration to: (1) the need for **affection** which involves acceptance and approval by persons; (2) the need for **belonging** which involves acceptance and approval of the group; and (3) the need for **mutuality** which involves cooperation, mutual helpfulness and group loyalty.

When it comes to evaluating social outcomes, we do not have the same kind of objective instruments that are available in computing accurately the physical attributes of children. In some cases (and primarily for diagnostic purposes) in their dealings with children, some school systems have successfully used some of the acceptable **sociometric** techniques. However, at best the social aspect is difficult to appraise objectively because of its somewhat vague nature.

Emotional Needs

In dealing with emotional needs, I repeat what was said earlier that we are confronted with the fact that for many years there have been many changing ideas and theories as far as the study of emotion is concerned. The degree to which emotional needs are met has considerable influence upon the development of the child's personality and upon mental health. Among the basic emotional needs are: (1) the need for a sense of security and trust; (2) the need for self-identity and self-respect; (3) the need for success, achievement and recognition; and (4) the need for independence.

The human personality is remarkably adaptive, and some children whose basic emotional needs are not met in one way or another are sometimes able to compensate in ways which still make for satisfactory mental health. For example, some orphan children learn to develop certain of their personality resources and thereby compensate for having received what in most people would be considered a lack of security. Still, the fact remains that beyond a certain point, if these emotional needs are not met, the child can easily develop emotional problems or personality disorders.

It is currently believed by many psychiatrists and psychologists that the foundation of mental health problems are laid in early childhood. Thus, it appears that adults play a major role in the development of "good" or "poor" mental health. Clearly, the obligations of adults (and particularly parents and teachers) are great in this matter of providing the home and school conditions that will encourage the forming of the basis of good mental health in the years to come. It is obvious that all children cannot intellectualize upon or evaluate their basic emotional needs. Most children react instinctively in seeking to meet their needs; thus, many facets of their personality and patterns of adjustment are being developed unconsciously. It is for this reason that most people do not know how they got many of their strong feelings about such things as jealousy, hostility, sex, religion and the like. At any rate, how children see themselves, other people of both sexes, and the world at large, and how they interpret and react to each of these, is molded and colored by their early experience.

When we attempt to evaluate the emotional aspect, we tend to encounter much the same situation as when we attempt to assess the social aspect, and the emotional aspect might well be more difficult to appraise than the social aspect. Among some of the methods used by researchers to attempt to measure emotional response are blood pressure, blood sugar analysis, pulse rate and galvanic skin response (a device somewhat like the lie detector apparatus). These methods and others that have been used by investigators of human emotion have various, and perhaps limited, degrees of validity. In attempting to assess emotional reactivity, investigators sometimes encounter problems in determining the extent to which they are dealing with a purely physiological response or a purely emotional response. Then, too, the type of emotional pattern is not identified by the measuring device. For example, a **joy** response and an **anger** response could show the same or nearly the same measure in microamperes when using a galvanic skin response device.

Intellectual Needs

Satisfactorily meeting children's intellectual needs is one of our greater concerns, as it is of paramount importance to success in school and life in general. There appears to be rather general agreement as to the intellectual needs of children. Among others, some of these needs include: (1) a need for challenging experiences at their own level; (2) a need for intellectually successful and satisfying experiences; (3) a need for the opportunity to solve problems; and (4) a need for opportunity to participate in creative experiences instead of always having to conform.

Assessment of the intellectual aspect is made by a variety of IQ tests. However, this should not always be considered a valid measurement of a child's intellectual ability, and many child psychologists tend to feel that this is more a measure of achievement than of basic intelligence. Incidentally, two of my associates on a childhood stress project, Bernard Brown of the Department of Health and Human Services and Lilian Rosenbaum of Georgetown University Medical Center,[1] have discovered that children who are under stress score 13 percent lower on intelligence tests than children who are not. (The work of these researchers will be discussed in Chapter 3.)

It can be concluded that when teachers and others have a better realization of the physical, social, emotional and intellectual needs of

---

[1] Bernard Brown and Lilian Rosenbaum, Stress and competence, in *Stress in Childhood,* ed. James H. Humphrey (New York AMS Press, Inc., 1984), pp. 127-154.

children, perhaps they can deal more satisfactorily with children in helping them with their life pursuits and to cope with undesirable psychological stress.

CHILDREN NEED TO
UNDERSTAND THEMSELVES

Among the various other struggles a child encounters in the process of growing and developing is that of gaining an understanding of **self.** It is the purpose of this section of the chapter to provide information that will help adults become more successful in their efforts to aid children in the process of self-realization.

In recent years there has been an increasing sentiment among young men and women of high school and college age that they have a need to **find** themselves. This should fortify the notion that one of the most important aspects of the "growing up" years is that children develop an understanding of themselves. This can be accomplished to some extent when adults improve upon their knowledge about growing children and, perhaps more important, being prepared to use this knowledge with children as they grow and develop.

As much as possible, parents and teachers should provide an environment in the home and in the school that is a stable sanctuary that the child knows will be there when needed. Children need to be accepted for themselves, with their own unique abilities and limitations. They need to be permitted to grow and learn at their own rate and in their own way — and not be made to feel inadequate in growing and learning even though they may not conform themselves to some standard or "norm." They need to identify themselves as distinct individuals, and their uniqueness is deserving of respect. As children mature, they should have the opportunity to assume independence and responsibilities that are commensurate with their age and abilities.

Children require control and discipline that is consistent, reasonable, and understandable to them. A few clear and simple rules are usually entirely adequate and tend to give children a feeling of security, in that they know what they can do and what they cannot do. Therefore, it may be said that children need defined limits to prevent them from destructive behavior and perhaps from even destroying themselves. It is important to emphasize that consistency in all aspects of the environment is very important. For example, acts for which they are ignored, praised, or punished should not vary from time to time. If they do, children are likely to become confused and their adjustments made more difficult. Similarly, expression of love should not be spasmodic, nor should the threat of withdrawal of love be used as an occasional weapon to control behavior.

Modern standard dictionaries ordinarily list almost 500 hyphenated words beginning with **self**—from **self**-abandonment to **self**-worth. The discussion here is going to be concerned with **self**-image, or how one conceives oneself or one's role. Reflecting back to the comments on physical development, recall the suggestion that where the child is concerned, **he is his body;** that is, he is essentially concerned with his **physical self.** It is something he can see and is much more meaningful to him than his social, emotional, and intellectual **self.** This being the case, attention is now turned to what will be called **body image,** which is the child's picture of his bodily person and his abilities. It has been clearly demonstrated that when teachers help children improve upon body image, then a basic understanding of the broader aspect of self will more likely be established.

Determining Deficiencies in Body Image

One of the first steps is to attempt to determine if a child has problems with body image. In this regard, it is doubtful that there is any absolutely foolproof method of detecting problems of body image in children. The reason for this is that many mannerisms said to be indicative of body-image problems can also be the same as for other deficiencies. Nevertheless, teachers should be alert to certain possible deficiencies.

Generally speaking, there are two ways in which deficiencies concerned with body image can be detected, at least in part, by observing certain behaviors. And, second, there are some relatively simple diagnostic techniques that can be used to determine such deficiencies. The following generalized list contains examples of both of these possibilities and is submitted to assist the reader in this particular regard:

1. One technique often used to diagnose possible problems of body image is to have children make a drawing of themselves. The primary reason for this is to see if certain parts of the body are **not** included in the drawing. My own personal experience as a Certified Binet Intelligence Test Examiner has revealed possibilities for such a diagnosis in the test item involving **picture completion.** In this test item a partial drawing of a "man" is provided for the child to complete. Since

the child's interest in drawing a man dates from his earliest attempts to represent things symbolically, it is possible, through typical drawings by young children, to trace certain characteristic stages of perceptual development. It has also been found in recent years that the procedure of drawing a picture of himself assists in helping to detect if there is a lack of body image.

2. Sometimes, the child with a lack of body image may manifest tenseness in his movements. At the same time, he may be unsure of his movements as he attempts to move the body segments.

3. If the child is instructed to move a body part such as placing one foot forward, he may direct his attention to the body part before making the movement. Or he may look at another child to observe the movement before he attempts to make the movement himself. This could also possibly be due to poor processing of the input (auditory or visual stimulus) provided for the movement.

4. When instructed to use one body part (arm), he may also move the corresponding body part (other arm) when it is not necessary. For example, he may be asked to swing the right arm and he may also start swinging the left arm simultaneously.

5. In such activities as catching an object, the child may turn toward the object when this is not necessary. For example, when a beanbag thrown to him approaches close to the child, he may move forward with either side of the body rather than trying to retrieve the beanbag with his hands while both feet remain stationary.

Improving Upon Body Image

In general, it might be said that when a child is given the opportunity to use his body freely in enjoyable movement, an increase in body image occurs. More specifically, there are activities that can be used in helping children identify and understand the use of various body parts, as well as the relationship of these parts.

Over a period of years, I have conducted a number of experiments in an attempt to determine the effect of participation in certain body-movement activities on body image. The following is an example of this approach, utilizing the game *Busy Bee*.

In this game, the children are in pairs facing each other and dispersed around the activity area. One child who is the **caller** is in the center of the area. This child makes calls, such as "shoulder to shoulder," "toe to toe," or "hand to hand." (In the early stages of the game, it might be a good idea for the teacher to do the calling.) As the calls are made, the paired children go through the appropriate motions with their partners. After a few calls, the caller will shout, "Busy Bee!" This is the signal for every child to get a new partner, including the caller. The child who does not get a partner can name the new caller.

This game has been experimented with in the following manner: As the children played the game, the teacher made them aware of the location of various parts of the body in order to develop the concept of full body image. Before the game was played, the children were asked to draw a picture of themselves. Many did not know how to begin, and others omitted some of the major limbs in their drawings. After playing Busy Bee, the children were asked again to draw a picture of themselves. This time they were more successful. All of the drawings had bodies, heads, arms, and legs. Some of them had hands, feet, eyes, and ears. A few even had teeth and hair.

Among the following activities will be found those that can be used for diagnosis for lack of body image, body-image improvement, evaluation of body-image status or various combinations of these factors. Some of the activities are age-old, while others have been developed for specific conditions.

Come With Me

Several children form a circle, with one child outside the circle. The child outside the circle walks around it, taps another child and says, "Come with me." The child tapped falls in behind the first child and they continue walking around the circle. The second child taps a child and says, "Come with me." This continues until several children have been tapped. At a given point the first child calls out, "Go home!" On this signal all the children try to get back to their original place in the circle. The first child also tries to get into one of these places. There will be one child left out. He can be the first child for the next game.

In the early stages of this game the teacher should call out where each child is to be tapped. For example, "on the arm," "on the leg," etc. After awhile, the child doing the tapping can call out where he is going to tap the child. The teacher can observe if children are tapped in the proper place.

Mirrors

One child is selected as the leader and stands in front of a line of children. This child goes through a variety of different movements and the children in the line try to do exactly the same thing; that is, they act as mirrors. The leader should be changed frequently.

In this activity, the children become aware of different body parts and movements as the child in front makes the various movements. The teacher should be alert to see how well and how quickly the children are able to do the movements that the child leader makes.

Change Circles

Several circles are drawn on the floor or outdoor activity area with one less circle than the number of participants. The one child who does not have a circle can be **It** and stands in the middle of the area. The teacher calls out signals in the form of body parts. For example, such calls could include: "hands on knees," "hands on head," "right hand on left foot," and so on. After a time, the teacher calls out, "Change circles!" whereupon all the children try to get into a different circle while the child who is **It** tries to find a circle. The child who does not find a circle can be **It** or a new person can be chosen to be **It.**

The teacher should observe closely to see how the children react to the calls and whether or not they are looking at the other children for clues. As time goes on and the children become more familiar with body parts, more complicated calls can be made.

Body Tag

In this game one child is selected to be **It.** He chases the other children and attempts to tag one of them. If he is successful, the child tagged can become **It.** If **It** does not succeed within a reasonable amount of time, a new **It** can be selected. In order to be officially tagged, a specific part of the body must be tagged by **It.** Thus, the game could be shoulder tag, arm tag, or leg tag as desired.

The teacher observes the child to see whether or not he tags the correct body part. To add more interest to the activity, the teacher can call out the part of the body to be tagged during each session of the game.

These activities are just a few of the possibilities for improving upon body image and, thus, an understanding of self. Creative teachers should be able to think of numerous activities that could satisfy this purpose.

Chapter 2

UNDERSTANDING CHILDHOOD EMOTIONS

EQUALLY IMPORTANT as an understanding of child development in teaching children to relax is an understanding of childhood emotions. At one time or another, all of us (children and teachers alike) demonstrate emotional behavior as well as ordinary behavior. Differences in the individual person and the environment will likely govern the extent to which each individual child will express emotional behavior.

Teachers should not necessarily think in terms of always suppressing the emotions of children. On the contrary, the goal should be to help children express their emotions as harmlessly as possible when they do occur so that emotional stability will be maintained. If this can be accomplished, the stress and tension resulting from harmful emotional behavior can at least be reduced, if not eliminated entirely.

Emotional stress can be brought about by the stimulus of any of the emotional patterns. For example, the emotional pattern of anger can be stimulated by such factors as the thwarting of one's wishes, or a number of cumulative irritations. Response to such stimuli can be either **impulsive** or **inhibited.** An impulsive expression of anger is one that is directed against a person or an object, while the inhibited expressions are kept under control and may be manifested by such overt behavior as skin flushing.

Generally speaking, emotional patterns can be placed into the two broad categories of **pleasant** emotions and **unpleasant** emotions. Pleasant emotional patterns can include such feelings as joy, affection, happiness, and love, while unpleasant emotional patterns can include anger, sorrow, jealousy, fear, and worry — an imaginary form of fear.

21

At one time or another all children manifest emotional behavior as well as ordinary behavior. Differences in the structure of the organism and in the environment will largely govern the degree to which each individual child expresses emotional behavior. Moreover, it has been suggested that the pleasantness or unpleasantness of an emotion seems to be determined by its strength or intensity, by the nature of the situation arousing it, and by the way the child perceives or interprets the situation.

The ancient Greeks identified emotions with certain organs of the body. For example, in general, sorrow was expressed from the heart (a broken heart), jealousy was associated with the liver, hate with the gallbladder, and anger with the spleen. In this regard, we sometimes hear the expression "venting the spleen" on someone. This historical reference is made, because in modern times we take into account certain conduits between the emotions and the body. These are by way of the nervous system and the endocrine system. That part of the nervous system principally concerned with the emotions is the **autonomic** nervous system which controls functions such as the heartbeat, blood pressure, and digestion. When there is a stimulus of any of the emotional patterns, these two systems activate. By way of illustration, if the emotional pattern of fear is stimulated, the heartbeat accelerates, breathing is more rapid, and the blood pressure is likely to rise. Energy fuel is discharged into the blood from storage in the liver, which causes the blood sugar level to rise. These, along with other bodily functions, serve to prepare a person for coping with the condition caused by the fear.

Dealing with childhood emotions implies that sympathetic guidance should be provided in meeting anxieties, joys, and sorrows, and that help should be given in developing aspirations and security. In order to attempt to reach this objective, we might well consider emotions from a standpoint of the growing child maturing emotionally.

For purposes of this discussion **maturity** will be considered as concerned with a state of **readiness** on the part of the organism. The term is most frequently used in connection with age relationships. For example, it may be said that "Johnny is mature for six years of age." Simply stated, **emotional maturity** is the process of acting one's age.

Generally speaking, emotional maturity will be achieved through a gradual accumulation of mild and pleasant emotions. Emotional **immaturity** indicates that unpleasant emotions have accumulated too rapidly for the child to absorb. One of the important factors in this regard is the process of **adjustment,** which can be described as the process of finding and adopting modes of behavior suitable to the environment or to changes in the environment.

The child's world involves a sequence of experiences that are characterized by the necessity for him to adjust. Consequently, it may be said that "normal" behavior is the result of successful adjustment and that abnormal behavior results from unsuccessful adjustment. The degree of adjustment that the child achieves depends upon how adequately he is able to satisfy his basic needs and to fulfill his desires within the framework of his environment and the pattern of ways dictated by society.

For purposes here, **stress** will be considered as any factor acting internally or externally that renders adaptation difficult and that induces increased effort on the person to maintain a state of equilibrium within himself and with his external environment. (In the following chapter, the stressfulness of the school environment will be dealt with in detail.)

When stress is induced as a result of the child's not being able to meet his needs (basic demands) and satisfy his desires (wants or wishes), **frustration** or **conflict** result. Frustration occurs when a need is not met, and conflict results when: (1) choices must be made between nearly equally attractive alternatives, or (2) when basic emotional forces oppose one another. In an emotionally healthy person, the degree of frustration is ordinarily in proportion to the intensity of the need or desire. That is, he will objectively observe and evaluate the situation to ascertain whether a solution is possible and, if so, what solution would best enable him to achieve the fulfillment of his needs or his desires.

Every person has a **zone of tolerance** or limit for emotional stress within which he normally operates. If the stress becomes considerably greater than the tolerance level or if the individual has not learned to cope with his problems and objectively and intelligently solve them, some degree of maladjustment can possibly result.

In order to counteract some of the above problems and to be able to pursue a sensible course in helping children become more emotionally mature, there are certain factors concerned with emotional development of children that need to be taken into account. Some of these factors are the subject of the ensuing discussion.

FACTORS CONCERNING EMOTIONAL DEVELOPMENT

Some of the factors concerned with emotional development of children that need to be considered are: (1) characteristics of childhood emotionality, (2) emotional arousals and reactions, and (3) factors that influence emotionality.

Characteristics of Childhood Emotionality

Ordinarily, the Emotions of Children Are Not Long Lasting

A child's emotions may last for a few minutes and then terminate rather abruptly. The child gets it "out of his system," so to speak, by expressing it outwardly. In contrast, some adult emotions may be long and drawn out. As children get older, expressing the emotions by overt action is encumbered by certain social restraints. This is to say that what might be socially acceptable at one age level is not necessarily so at another. This may be a reason for some children developing **moods,** which in a sense are states of emotion drawn out over a period of time and expressed slowly. Typical moods of childhood may be "sulking" due to restraint of anger, being "jumpy" from repressed fear, and becoming "humorous" from controlled joy or happiness.

The Emotions of Children Are Likely to Be Intense

This might be confusing to some adults who do not understand child behavior. That is, they may not be able to see why a child would react rather violently to a situation that to them might appear insignificant.

The Emotions of Children Are Subject to Rapid Change

A child is capable of shifting rapidly from laughing to crying or from anger to joy. Although the reason for this is not definitely known, it might be that there is not as much depth of feeling among children as there is among adults. In addition, it could be due to lack of experience that children have had, as well as their state of intellectual development. We know that young children have a short attention span that could cause them to change rapidly from one kind of emotion to another.

The Emotions of Children Can Appear With a High Degree of Frequency

As children get older they manage to develop the ability to adjust to situations that previously would have caused an emotional reaction. This is probably due to the child's acquiring more experience with various kinds of emotional situations. Perhaps a child learns through experience what is socially acceptable and what is socially unacceptable. This is particularly true if the child is reprimanded in some way following a violent emotional reaction. For this reason, the child may try to confront situations in ways that do not involve an emotional response.

Children Differ in Their Emotional Responses

One child confronted with a situation that instills fear may run away from the immediate environment. Another may hide behind his mother. Still another might just stand there and cry. Different reactions of children to emotional situations are probably due to a host of factors. Included among these may be past experiences with a certain kind of emotional situation, willingness of parents and other adults to help children become independent, and family relationships in general.

Strength of Children's Emotions
Are Subject to Change

At some age levels certain kinds of emotions may be weak and later become stronger. Conversely, with some children emotions that were strong may tend to decline. For example, small children may be timid among strangers, but later, when they see there is nothing to fear, the timidity is likely to wane.

Emotional Arousals and Reactions

If we are to understand the emotions of children, we need to take into account those factors of emotional arousal and how children might be expected to react to them. Many different kinds of emotional patterns have been identified. For purposes here, I have arbitrarily selected for discussion the emotional states of fear, worry, anger, jealousy, and joy.

Fear

It is possible that it is not necessarily the arousal itself but rather the way something is presented that determines whether there will be a fear reaction. For example, if a child is trying to perform a stunt and the discussion is in terms of "if you do it that way you will break your neck," it is possible a fear response will occur. This is one of the many reasons for using a positive approach in dealing with children.

A child may react to fear by withdrawing. With very young children, this may be in the form of crying or breath holding. With a child under three years of age (and in some older children as well), the "ostrich" approach may be used; that is, he may hide his face in order to get away from it. As children get older, these forms of reactions may decrease or cease altogether because of social pressures. For instance, it may be considered "sissy" to cry, especially among boys. (The validity of this kind of thinking is of course open to question.)

Worry

This might be considered an imaginary form of fear and it can be a fear not aroused directly from the child's environment. Worry can be aroused by imagining a situation that could possibly arise; that is, a child could worry about not being able to perform well in a certain activity. Since worries are likely to be caused by imaginary rather than real conditions, they are not likely to be found in abundance among young children. Perhaps the reason for this is that a very young child has not reached the stage of intellectual development at which he or she might imagine certain things that could cause worry. While children will respond to worry in different ways, certain manifestations such as nail biting may be symptomatic of this condition.

Anger

This emotional response tends to occur more frequently than that of fear. This is probably because there are more conditions that incite anger. In addition, some children quickly learn that anger may get attention that otherwise would not be forthcoming. It is likely that as children get older they may show more anger responses than fear responses because they soon see that there is not much to fear.

Anger is caused by many factors, one of which is interference with movements that a child may want to execute. This interference can come from others or by the child's own limitations in ability and physical development.

Because of individual differences in children, there is a wide variation in anger responses. As mentioned previously, these responses are either **impulsive** or **inhibited.** In impulsive responses, the child manifests an overt action either toward another person or an object that caused the anger. For instance, a child who collides with a door might take out the anger by kicking or hitting the door. (This form of child behavior is also sometimes manifested by some "adults.") Inhibited responses are likely to be kept under control, and as children mature emotionally, they acquire more ability to control their anger.

Jealousy

This response usually occurs when a child feels a threat of loss of affection. Many psychologists believe that jealousy is closely related to anger. Because of this, the child may build up resentment against another person. Jealousy can be devastating in childhood and every effort should be made to avoid it.

Jealousy is concerned with social interaction that involves persons the child likes. These individuals can be parents, siblings, teachers, and peers. There are various ways in which the child may respond. These include: (1) being aggressive toward the one of whom one is jealous or possibly toward others as well, (2) withdrawing from the person whose affections he thinks have been lost, and (3) possible development of an "I-don't-care" attitude.

In some cases children will not respond in any of the above ways. They might try to excel over the person of whom they are jealous or they might tend to do things to impress the person whose affections they thought had been lost.

Joy

This pleasant emotion is one for which we strive because it is so important in maintaining emotional stability. Causes of joy differ from one age level to another and from one child to another at the same age level. This is to say that what might be joyful for one person might not necessarily be so for another.

Joy is expressed in various ways, but the most common are laughing and smiling, the latter being a restrained form of laughter. Some people respond to joy with a state of relaxation. This is difficult to detect, because it has little or no overt manifestations. Nevertheless, it may be noticed when one compares it with body tension caused by unpleasant emotion.

Factors That Influence Emotionality

If we can consider that a child is emotionally fit when his emotions are properly controlled and he is becoming emotionally mature, then emotional fitness is dependent to a certain extent upon certain factors that influence emotionality in childhood. The following is a descriptive list of some of these factors.

Fatigue

There are two types of fatigue: **acute** and **chronic.** Acute fatigue is a natural outcome of sustained severe exertion. It is due to physical factors such as the accumulation of the by-products of muscular exertion in the blood and to excessive **oxygen debt** — the ability of the body to take in as much oxygen as is being consumed by the muscular work. Psychological considerations may also be important in acute fatigue. That is, an individual who becomes bored with his work and who becomes preoccupied with the discomfort involved will become "fatigued" much sooner than if he is highly motivated to do the same work, is not bored, and does not think about the discomfort.

Chronic fatigue refers to fatigue that lasts over extended periods, in contrast to acute fatigue, which tends to be followed by a recovery phase and restoration to "normal" within a more or less brief period of time. Chronic fatigue may be due to any or a variety of medical conditions ranging from a disease to malnutrition. (Such conditions are the concern of the physician, who, incidentally, should evaluate all cases of chronic fatigue in order to assure that a disease condition is not responsible.) It may also be due to psychological factors such as extreme boredom and/or worry of having to do what one does not wish to do over an extended period.

Fatigue predisposes children to irritability; consequently, actions are taken to ward it off, such as having rest periods or, in the case of the nursery school, fruit juice periods. In this particular regard, some studies show that the hungrier a child is, the more prone he may be to outbursts of anger.

Inferior Health Status

The same thing holds true here as in the case of fatigue. Temporary poor health, such as colds and the like, tend to make children irritable. There are studies that show that there are fewer emotional outbursts among healthy than unhealthy children.

Intelligence

Studies tend to show that, on the average, children of low intellectual levels have less emotional control than children with higher levels of intelligence. This may be because there may be less frustration if a child is intelligent enough to figure things out. The reverse could also be true, because children with high levels of intelligence are better able to perceive things that would be likely to arouse emotions.

Social Environment

In a social environment where such things as quarreling and unrest exist, a child is predisposed to unpleasant emotional conditions. Likewise, school schedules that are too crowded can cause undue emotional excitation among children.

Family Relationships

There are a variety of conditions concerned with family relationships that can influence childhood emotionality. Among others, these include: (1) parental neglect, (2) overanxious parents, and (3) overprotective parents.

Aspiration Levels

It can make for an emotionally unstable situation if parent expectations are beyond a child's ability. In addition, children who have not been made aware of their own limitations may set goals too high and as a result have too many failures.

All of these factors can have a negative influence on childhood emotionality and, thus, possibly induce emotional stress. Therefore, efforts should be made as far as possible to eliminate the negative aspects of these factors. Those that cannot be completely eliminated should at least be kept under control.

GUIDELINES FOR EMOTIONAL DEVELOPMENT OF CHILDREN

It is imperative to set forth some guidelines for emotional development if we are to meet with any degree of success in our attempts to provide for emotional development of children. The reason for this is to assure, at least to some extent, that our efforts in attaining optimum emotional development will be based upon a scientific approach. These guidelines might well be taken in the form of valid **concepts of emotional development.** This approach enables us to give serious consideration to what is known about how children grow and develop. The following list of concepts of emotional development with certain implications for the school environment is submitted with this general idea in mind.

1. **An emotional response may be brought about by a goal's being furthered or thwarted.** The teacher should make a very serious effort to assure successful experiences in the school for every child. This can be accomplished in part by attempting to provide for individual differences within given school experiences. The school setting should be such that each child derives a feeling of personal worth through making some sort of positive contribution.

2. **Self-realization experiences should be constructive.** The opportunity for creative experiences that afford the child a chance for self-realization should be inherent in school. Teachers might well consider planning with children to see that all school activities are meeting their needs and, as a result, involve constructive experiences.

3. **Emotional responses increase as the development of the child brings greater awareness and the ability to remember the past and to anticipate the future.** In the school setting the teacher can remind the children of their past pleasant emotional responses with words of praise. This could encourage children to repeat such responses later in similar situations and thus provide a better learning situation.

4. **As the child develops, the emotional reactions tend to become less violent and more discriminating.** A well-planned program of school experiences and wholesome home activities should be such that it provides for release of aggression in a socially acceptable manner.

5. **Emotional reactions tend to increase beyond normal expectancy toward the constructive or destructive reactions on the balance of furthering or hindering experiences of the child.** For some children the confidence they need to be able to face the problems of life may come through physical expression. Therefore, experiences such as good physical education programs in the schools have tremendous potential to help contribute toward a solid base of total development.

6. **Depending on certain factors, a child's own feelings may be accepted or rejected by the individual.** Children's school experiences should make them feel good and have confidence in themselves. Satisfactory self-concept is closely related to body control; physical activity-oriented experiences might be considered as one of the best ways of contributing to it. Therefore, it is important to consider those kinds of experiences for children that will provide them with the opportunity for a certain degree of freedom of movement.

OPPORTUNITIES FOR EMOTIONAL DEVELOPMENT IN THE SCHOOL ENVIRONMENT

The school has the potential to provide for emotional stability. The extent to which this actually occurs is dependent primarily on the kind of emotional climate provided by the teacher. For this reason, it appears pertinent to examine some of the potential opportunities that exist for emotional development in the school situation. It should be borne in mind that these opportunities will not accrue automatically, but that teachers need to work constantly to try to make such conditions a reality.

1. **Release of aggression in a socially acceptable manner.** This appears to be an outstanding way in which school activities such as physical education can help to make children more secure and emotionally stable. For example, kicking a ball in a game of kickball, batting a softball, or engaging in a combative stunt can afford a socially acceptable way of releasing aggression.

2. **Inhibition of direct response of unpleasant emotions.** This statement does not necessarily mean that feelings concerned with such unpleasant emotions as fear and anger should be completely restrained. On the contrary, the interpretation should be that such feelings can take place less frequently in a wholesome school environment. This means that opportunities should be provided to relieve tension rather than aggravate it, the major purpose of this book.

3. **Promotion of pleasant emotions.** Perhaps there is too much concern with suppressing unpleasant emotions and not enough attention given to promoting the pleasant ones. This means that the school should provide a range of activities by which all children can succeed. Thus, all children, regardless of ability, should be afforded the opportunity for success, at least some of the time.

4. **Recognition of one's abilities and limitations.** It has already been mentioned that a wide range of activities should provide an opportunity for success for all. This should make it easier in the school setting to provide for individual differences of children so that all of them can progress within the limits of their own skill and ability.

5. **Understanding about the ability and achievements of others.** In the school experience emphasis can be placed upon achievements of the group, along with the function of each individual in the group. Team play and group effort is important in most school situations.

6. Being able to make a mistake without being ostracized. In the school setting this requires that the teacher serve as a catalyst who helps children understand the idea of trial and error. Emphasis can be placed on **trying** and on the fact that one can learn not only from his own mistakes but also from the mistakes of others.

This discussion has included just a few examples of the numerous opportunities to help provide for emotional development in the school environment. The resourceful and creative teacher should be able to expand this list manyfold.

IMPLICATIONS OF RESEARCH IN EMOTIONAL BEHAVIOR OF CHILDREN

Over the years, attempts have been made to study various aspects of childhood emotions. One such undertaking by the National Institute of Education provides some information that might be useful.[1]

The purpose of this report was to provide preschool and early elementary school teachers with a summary of current psychological research concerned with the social development of young children. In submitting the report, the authors noted that caution should prevail with reference to basic research and practical implications. In this regard, the following suggestions are submitted:

1. What seems "true" at one point often becomes "false" when new information becomes available or when new theories change the interpretation of the old findings.
2. Substantial problems arise in any attempt to formulate practical suggestions for professionals in one discipline based on research findings from another discipline.
3. Throughout the report, recommendations for teachers have been derived from logical extensions of experimental findings and classroom adaptations of experimental procedures.
4. Some of the proposed procedures may prove unworkable in the classroom, even though they may make sense from a psychological perspective.
5. When evaluating potential applications of psychological findings, it is important to remember that psychological research is usually

---

[1] W.R. Roedell, G. Slaby and H.B. Robinson, *Social Development in Young Children* (Washington, DC, National Institute of Education, January, 1976).

designed to derive probability statements about the behavior of groups of people.

6. Individual teachers may work better with a procedure that is, on the average, less effective.

The following is a list of generalizations derived from the findings of the study of **aggression** in children and is accompanied by possible general implications for the school environment. These implications are suggestive only, and the reader will no doubt be able to draw his or her own implications and make practical applications that apply to particular situations.

1. Children rewarded for aggression learn that aggression pays off. This generalization is concerned with the extent to which a teacher uses praise for achievement. The teacher must be able to discern quickly whether success was due more to aggressive behavior than skill or ability. The important thing here is the extent of aggressive behavior. Certainly, a teacher should not thwart enthusiasm. It is sometimes difficult to determine whether an act was due to genuine enthusiasm or to overt, undesirable, aggressive behavior.

2. Children involved in constructive activities may be less likely to behave aggressively. In the school setting, this implies that lessons should be well-planned so that time is spent on constructive learning activities. When this is accomplished, it will be more likely that desirable and worthwhile learning will take place.

3. Children who have alternative responses readily available are less likely to resort to aggression to get what they want. This is concerned essentially with teacher-child relationships. While the school environment involves group situations, there are many "one-on-one" opportunities between teacher and child. This gives the teacher a chance to verbalize to the child the kind of behavior that is expected under certain conditions. For example, a child who **asks** for an object such as a ball is more likely to receive cooperation. A child who **grabs** an object is more likely to elicit retaliatory aggression. Teaching reinforcement can increase children's use of non-aggressive solutions to interpersonal problems.

The teacher should be ready to intervene in a potentially aggressive situation before aggression occurs, encouraging children to use non-aggressive methods to solve conflicts. The teacher can provide verbal alternatives for those children who do not think of them. For example, "I am playing with this now," or "You can ask him to trade with you."

4. Children imitate behavior of people they like, and they often adopt a teacher's behavior. Teachers are more likely to be a model adopted by children than would be the case of most other adults, sometimes including parents. One of the reasons is that many children like to try to please their teachers and tend to make serious efforts to do so. Of course, it is helpful if a teacher is non-aggressive in his or her own behavior.

5. Cooperation may be incompatible with aggression. This could be interpreted to mean that a teacher should consistently attend to and reinforce all cooperative behavior. Children consistently reinforced for cooperative behavior are likely to increase cooperative interactions while simultaneously decreasing aggressive behavior.

EVALUATING INFLUENCES OF THE SCHOOL ENVIRONMENT ON EMOTIONAL DEVELOPMENT

What we are essentially concerned with here is how an individual teacher can make some sort of valid evaluation of the extent to which the school environment is contributing to emotional development. This means that the teacher should make some attempt to assess school experiences with reference to whether or not these experiences are providing for emotional maturity.

One approach would be to refer back to the list of opportunities for emotional development in the school environment suggested previously. These opportunities have been converted into a rating scale as follows and may be used by the teacher:

1. The school experience provides for release of aggression in a socially acceptable manner.
      4   most of the time
      3   some of the time
      2   occasionally
      1   infrequently

2. The school experiences provide for inhibition of direct response to unpleasant emotions.
      4   most of the time
      3   some of the time
      2   occasionally
      1   infrequently

3. The school experiences provide for promotion of pleasant emotions.
   - 4 most of the time
   - 3 some of the time
   - 2 occasionally
   - 1 infrequently

4. The school experiences provide for recognition of one's abilities and limitations.
   - 4 most of the time
   - 3 some of the time
   - 2 occasionally
   - 1 infrequently

5. The school experiences provide for an understanding about the ability and achievement of others.
   - 4 most of the time
   - 3 some of the time
   - 2 occasionally
   - 1 infrequently

6. The school experiences provide for being able to make a mistake without being ostracized.
   - 4 most of the time
   - 3 some of the time
   - 2 occasionally
   - 1 infrequently

If a teacher makes these ratings objectively and conscientiously, a reasonably good procedure for evaluation is provided. Ratings can be made periodically to see if positive changes appear to be taking place. Ratings can be made for a single experience, a group of experiences, or for the total school environment. This procedure can help the teacher identify the extent to which school experiences and/or conditions under which the experiences take place are contributing to emotional development, and thus to the control of emotional stress and tension.

THE EMOTIONALLY HEALTHY PERSON

It seems appropriate to close this chapter by mentioning some of the characteristics of emotionally healthy persons. Looking at these characteristics we must recognize that they are not absolute nor static. We are not always happy, and we sometimes find ourselves in situations where we are not overly confident. In fact, sometimes we may feel downright inadequate to solve commonplace problems that occur in our daily lives.

1. The emotionally healthy person has achieved basic harmony within himself or herself and a workable relationship with others. He or she is able to function effectively, and usually happily, even though well aware of the limitations and rigors involved in human existence.

2. The emotionally healthy person manages to adapt to the demands of environmental conditions with emotional responses that are appropriate in degree and kind to the stimuli and situations and that fall, generally, within the range of what is considered "normal" within various environments.

3. The emotionally healthy person faces problems directly and seeks realistic and plausible solutions to them. Such a person tries to free himself or herself from excessive and unreal anxieties, worries, and fears, even though there is an awareness that there is much to be concerned with and much to be anxious about in our complex modern society.

4. The emotionally healthy person has developed a guiding philosophy of life and has a set of values that are acceptable to one and that are generally acceptable with those values of society that are reasonable and conducive to human happiness.

5. The emotionally healthy person accepts himself or herself and is willing to deal with the world as it exists in reality. He or she accepts what cannot be changed at a particular time and place and builds and derives satisfaction within the framework of his or her own potentialities and those of the environment.

6. The emotionally healthy person tends to be happy and to have an enthusiasm for living. He or she does not focus attention exclusively upon what is considered to be inadequacies, weaknesses, and "bad" qualities. Such a person views those around him or her this way, too.

7. The emotionally healthy person has a variety of satisfying interests and maintains a balance between work, routine responsibilities, and recreation. Constructive and satisfying outlets for creative expression are found in the interests undertaken.

This list of characteristics of the emotionally healthy person presents a near-ideal situation, and obviously none of us operates at these high levels at all times. However, they might well be considered as suitable guidelines for which we might strive to help us deal with and possibly prevent unpleasant emotional stress and tension, not only for ourselves but for the children we deal with, as well.

Chapter 3

STRESS IN THE
SCHOOL ENVIRONMENT

T HE NEED FOR periodic relaxation activities in the school day is evidenced by the stress, anxiety and tension prevailing in many school environments. Indeed, there are a number of conditions existing in many school situations that can cause much stress and tension for children. In this regard, Thoresen and Eagleston[1] have discussed the consequences of experiencing prolonged chronic stress for students in the education system, from preschool to graduate school. They believe that the child or adolescent who is facing a set of demands with insufficient resources may respond in many ways that are harmful or maladaptive.

Miscoping responses can include behavioral and environmental responses such as social withdrawal, alcohol or drug abuse, and truancy. In the cognitive area, an imbalance of demands and resources could result in feelings of low self-esteem and beliefs about being a failure. Related to these is the possible evolution of "learned helplessness," the belief that one's actions essentially are unrelated to the consequences that are experienced. Strategies for overcoming chronic stress, such as physical exercise and the learning of new social skills, are highly recommended by these authors.

STRESS AND THE CHILD
IN THE EDUCATIVE PROCESS

School anxiety as a child stressor is a phenomenon with which educators, particularly teachers and counselors, frequently find themselves

---

[1] C.E. Thoresen and J.R. Eagleston, Chronic stress in children and adolescents, *Theory into Practice* 22 (1983): 48-56.

confronted in dealing with children. Various theories have been advanced to explain this phenomenon and relate it to other character traits and emotional dispositions. Literature on the subject reveals the following characteristics of anxiety as a stress inducing factor in the educative process.

1. Anxiety is considered a learnable reaction that has the properties of a response, a cue of danger, and a drive.
2. Anxiety is internalized fear aroused by the memory of painful past experiences associated with punishment for the gratification of an impulse.
3. Anxiety in the classroom interferes with learning, and whatever can be done to reduce it should serve as a spur to learning.
4. Test anxiety is a near-universal experience, especially in this country, which is a test-giving and test-conscious culture.
5. Evidence from clinical studies points clearly and consistently to the disruptive and distracting power of anxiety effects over most kinds of thinking.

It would seem that causes of anxiety change with age as do perceptions of stressful situations. Care should be taken in assessing the total life space of the child—background, home life, school life, age, and sex—in order to minimize the anxiety experienced in the school. It seems obvious that school anxiety, although manifested in the school environment, may often be caused by unrelated factors outside the school.

Conners[2] studied certain interactions with the educative process as they relate to stress. He discussed growing evidence that the designed environment of schools may stress users of the facility both directly and indirectly. Several areas where the designed environment, both on a school-wide and classroom level, interacts with the educational process were explored, and these interactions were considered from the perspective of stresses imposed on both teacher and student. Seating position, classroom design and arrangement, density and crowding, privacy, and noise were considered. He suggests that schools need to provide places that will enhance goals of interaction, for participation in social networks, and for control over the time and place for social interactions. Relatively minor design modifications introduced into already functioning classrooms have been shown to produce changes in students' spatial behavior, increased interaction with materials, and decreased interruption.

---

[2] D.A. Conners, The school environment: A link to understanding stress, *Theory into Practice* 22 (1983): 15-20.

Obviously, cognitive behaviors are important in the educative process and for success in school. In this regard, Houston, Fox and Forbes[3] studied this factor as it was concerned with children's state anxiety and performance under stress. They evaluated the relations between trait anxiety in children and state anxiety, cognitive behaviors, and performance in a single study in which two levels of stress were experimentally manipulated.

Sixty-seven fourth grade children (41 females, 26 males) anticipated and then performed a mathematics task in either a high- or a low-stress condition. While the children anticipated performing the task, measures of 7 cognitive behaviors were obtained by means of a think-aloud procedure and a cognitive behavior questionnaire. The children were also administered the State-Trait Anxiety Inventory for Children. Trait anxiety was found to be related to the state anxiety and the cognitive behaviors of preoccupation and, for females, justification of positive attitudes. The performance of high but not low trait-anxious children was affected by levels of success. This finding aids in reconciling discrepancies in previous research concerning children's trait anxiety and performance.

In another study, Barton[4] examined behavioral stability of elementary school children and the effect of environmental stress. She assessed the stability of social behavior, academic performance and study skills in 130 elementary school children over a period of 2 to 4 years. The impact of stressful life events on behavioral stability, and the nature of particularly potent stressors were also investigated.

Children were aged 6, 7 and 8 years at the time of the initial assessment and were drawn from primarily intact, white families in a middle-class community. The data included academic grades, conduct ratings in four general areas (work skills, social skills, behavior and independent thought), and standardized test scores taken from school records. Peer and teacher ratings were also obtained when the children were aged 8, 9 and 10 years. The Life Events Record, a measure of stressful life events occurring in a given year, was administered to parents in telephone interviews.

The results indicated an impressive degree of stability in both social behavior and academic performance in the middle elementary school years with stability coefficients increasing with the age of the

---

[3] B. Houston, J.E. Fox, and L. Forbes, Trait anxiety and children's state anxiety, cognitive behaviors, and performance under stress, *Cognitive Therapy and Research* 8 (1984): 631-641.

[4] M. Barton, "Behavior stability in the elementary school years and the effects of environmental stress" (Doctoral diss., University of Connecticut, Storrs, CT, 1983).

child at the initial assessment. Increases in the frequency of stressful life events appeared related to lower ratings of academic performance, but were unrelated to ratings of social behavior when these were assessed concurrently. High levels of stress experienced earlier in a child's history showed little relationship to social behaviors but did exert a facilitative influence on academic performance and study skills. A subscale of the Life Events Record composed solely of negative events was most strongly related to behavioral changes; the dimension of controllability of events was unrelated to the potency of life stressors. Familial background and a child's earlier performance levels appeared to be important mediators of children's behavioral responses to stressful life events.

If the child is to be successful in the educative process, it is imperative that he or she be able to make the best use of native intelligence. The fact that stress can have a negative impact on IQ and task performance is shown in the work of Brown and Rosenbaum,[5] two eminent researchers on the subject. The following discussion consists of some of the excerpted materials of their work in this field.

They examined the effects of stress on IQ in a sample of 4,154 of 41,540 7-year-old children from the Collaborative Project. They developed a stress index which was a composite score of the number of medical/psychological problems found in a child. The variables were selected from the Collaborative Project data files collected in the 1960s. They included mother's marital status, employment, family configuration, history of illness, death, and divorce in the family, measures of autonomic function, achievement measures and physician-identified health disorders including vision, motor, speech, and hearing problems. They found an inverted-U curve of performance on the WISC IQ test and its component subtests for IQ vs. stress level as measured by total number of problems per child. For example, on the WISC Information subtest, white middle-class children with 3 problems scored the equivalent of 8 IQ points higher than those with no problems and 13 points higher than those with 10 problems. The Information, Block Design, and Coding subtests have the greatest sensitivity to stress, and the Comprehension and Vocabulary subtests were the least sensitive. The inverted-U curve of the full-scale WISC IQ test was less pronounced than the curves of the subtests, with only a 7-point difference between maximum performance level and the performance level under high

---

[5] B. Brown and L. Rosenbaum, Stress and competence, chap. 7 in *Stress in Childhood*, ed. James H. Humphrey (New York, AMS Press, Inc., 1984), pp. 127-154.

stress. The curves of low-SES children were of the same inverted-U form but were peaked at lower stress levels, suggesting higher arousal and stressor levels. Thus, the researchers showed that stress has a large effect on intelligence test scores.

On the basis of their work and a review of the literature, they have put forward a body of evidence to support the hypothesis that stress affects intelligence. They presented evidence that many families are exposed to high stressor levels, both acute and chronic. Stress affects the level of anxiety, sense of mastery, self-esteem, depression, and general ability to function in the family which in turn shapes children's competence. Stressors influence performance, both immediately and developmentally, as they interact with genetics, environment, and experience to shape physical, social, emotional and intellectual growth.

They have also presented evidence that acute stressors disrupt the balance between cognitive and emotional function as highly differentiated thought decreases and the brain becomes emotionally overreactive. Children who experience chronic stressors, either real or perceived, show a long-term decline in intelligence if their coping skills are inadequate, while children with appropriate coping skills rise in intelligence.

They suggest that the hypothesis that stress affects competence implies a different set of interventions in dealing with dysfunction in children and families. Competence in functioning can be altered by modifying the degree of individual differentiation, the intensity, frequency, and predictability of the stressor, and/or the individual's response (arousal) to the stressors and processes of family function. These interpretations can alter the present competence of the individual as well as presumably counter the transmission of suboptimal functioning across generations. These include education in family processes and/or therapy as well as training in a variety of self-regulation techniques such as biofeedback and stress management. There are ways to increase the number of stress-resisting factors to protect children from unnecessary risk. There can be intervention in schools and other organizations to insure that organizational processes do not lead to overreactivity in children and families.

THE STRESSFULNESS OF SCHOOL ADJUSTMENT

One of the most stressful of life events for young children is beginning the first grade. One of the reasons for this may possibly be that older childhood friends, siblings and even some unthinking parents admonish the child with "wait until you get to school—you're going to get it." This kind of negative attitude is likely to increase any "separation anxiety" that the child already has.

Such separation anxiety begins in the first stage of the child's development, from birth to 15 months. It can reach a peak in the latter part of the developmental stage from 3 to 5 years because it is the first attempt to become a part of the outer world—the school. For many children this is the first task of enforced separation. For those who do not have a well-developed sense of continuity, the separation might be easily equated with the loss of the life-sustaining mother. The stress associated with such a disaster could be overwhelming for such a child. Learning to tolerate the stress of separation is one of the central concerns of preschoolers; adults should be alert to signs and seek to lessen the impact. Compromises should be worked out, not necessarily to remove the stress, but to help the child gradually build a tolerance for separation.

It has been suggested by Chandler[6] that in extreme cases of the separation problem, a child's reaction typically may include temper tantrums, crying, screaming, and downright refusal to go to school. Or, in some cases, suspiciously sudden aches and pains might serve to keep the "sick" child home. What the child is reacting against is not the school but separation from the mother. The stress associated with this event may be seen by the child as a devastating loss equated with being abandoned. The child's behavior in dealing with the stress can be so extreme as to demand special treatment on the part of the significant adults in his or her life.

The aim in such cases should always be to ease the transition into school. It is important to keep in mind that separation is a two-way street. Assuring parents of the competency of the school staff and of the physical safety of their child may go a long way toward helping to lessen the stress. If adults act responsibly and with consistence, the child should be able to make an adequate adjustment to this daily separation from family and, in the process, learn an important lesson in meeting reality demands.

Several studies concerning stress and school adjustment have been conducted in recent years and some representative examples of these follow.

Kaufman[7] studied the stress and coping styles of elementary school children. She reviewed research literature related to the topic of stressors

---

[6] L.A. Chandler, *Children Under Stress* (Springfield, IL, Charles C Thomas, Publisher, 1982), p. 26.

[7] S.S. Kaufman, "Stresses and coping styles of elementary school children" (Doctoral diss., Arizona State University, Tempe, AZ, 1984).

in the lives of elementary school-aged children. The literature revealed that the history of research on stress focused on the identification of significant life events and the physiological and affective responses of stress. The relationship between life events and the responses to stress has been studied, as has the effect of specific social circumstances, coping styles and developmental status in the measurement of stress in children.

To add to the literature on stress and children, three elementary school-aged children in a suburban area in the southwestern United States were observed and interviewed to ascertain some of the significant life events contributing to their presumed difficulty in **school adjustment.** The three children were concluding their third grade academic year when first identified and were observed during the first half of fourth grade. Extensive observations and interviews with teachers, parents, and other significant people in the children's lives were collected. This information and direct interviews with two of the three children constituted the main source of the data in this naturalistic research study.

Data collection and analysis procedures followed the theoretical orientation of grounded theory. A substantive theory regarding the stressors in the lives of the three children was produced. Within the classroom, the theory proposed that classroom noise levels, teacher correction of a child's behavior, and the pressure placed on a child to perform in class may have contributed to the stress experienced by the children. Other classroom-related stressors included peer correction of classwork, the allotted physical space and territory of children, the excessively hot temperature in the classroom, peer usage of pejorative name-calling and the use of external behavior reward systems. Finally, the theory proposed that boredom or disinterest in the school curriculum, the process of socialization and peer relationships may have affected the children. Within the home environment the potential sources of stress identified in this study included strained rapport with siblings and/or parents, parental pressures to participate in activities outside the home and history of child neglect and abuse.

Sterling[8] examined the recent stressful life events and young children's school adjustment. A total of 211 first–fourth graders who had experienced one or more stressful life events (SLEs) were compared to a demographically matched sample of 211 children who had not experienced SLEs on measures of school adjustment problems and competencies.

---

[8] S. Sterling, Recent stressful life events and young children's school adjustment, *American Journal of Community Psychology* 13 (1985): 87-98.

The children's teachers completed the Classroom Adjustment Rating Scale, the Health Resources Inventory, and a 40-item measure of SLEs, background, and personal characteristics for each child. SLEs were found to be associated with the presence of more serious school adjustment problems and fewer competencies. Those associations were strongest for children who had experienced multiple recent SLEs. The importance of preventive interventions for this at-risk group was emphasized.

Stress of young children transferring to new schools was studied by Field.[9] Fourteen preschool children who were transferring to new schools were observed during a two-week period prior to the separation from their 14 classmates who were not transferring. The children ranged in age from 2.9 to 5 years. They were interviewed with the Piers-Harris Children's Self-Concept Scale and the Depression Rating Scale for Children. Parents and teachers completed questionnaires on child behavior. Results showed that children leaving the school, compared to those who were staying, showed increases (compared to baseline observations three months earlier) in fantasy play, physical contact, negative statements and affect, fussiness, activity level, tonic heart rate, and illness, as well as changes in eating and sleeping patterns. Shortly after their departure, this agitated behavior appeared to diminish in the children who were leaving but increased for those who remained in the school. This behavior pattern may represent a coping response to separation in an environment that is laden with cues of losses associated with separation.

In a similar study Blair, Marchant and Medway[10] considered the problem of aiding the relocated family and mobile child. They were concerned with methods that have proved successful in integrating mobile students into a new school, and they provided an overview of a program developed by them to help highly mobile families deal with moving-related stress.

A summer visitation program was designed to meet the social and emotional needs of entering students by making the family more aware of school policies, developing lines of communication between the family and school, and welcoming the family into the community. The program of Students Assimilated into Learning was designed to aid large numbers of mobile children, with an emphasis on remediation. Other techniques

---

[9] T. Field, Separation stress for young children transferring to new schools, *Developmental Psychology* 20 (1984): 786-792.

[10] J.P. Blair, K.H. Marchant, and F.J. Medway, Aiding the relocated family and mobile child, *Elementary School Guidance and Counseling* 18 (1984): 251-259.

for aiding mobile children included entrance interviews, orientation cycles, and mobility groups. The project of these researchers was directed at parents stationed at a large military base and was designed to sensitize parents about children's feelings about moving and the ways they may express those feelings. Concrete suggestions for helping children with moving were included.

STRESS AND COMPETITION IN THE SCHOOL ENVIRONMENT

In a study conducted with 200 fifth and sixth grade children one of the questions asked was "What is the one thing that worries you most in school?"[11] As might be expected, there were a variety of responses. However, the one general characteristic that tended to emerge was the emphasis placed on **competition** in so many school situations. Although students did not state this specifically, the nature of their responses clearly seemed to be along these lines.

Most of the literature on competition for children has focused on sports activities; however, there are many situations that exist in some classrooms that can cause **competitive stress.** An example is the antiquated "spelling bee" which still exists in some schools and, in fact, continues to be recognized in an annual national competition. Perhaps the first few children "spelled down" are likely to be the ones who need spelling practice the most. And, to say the least, it can be embarrassing in front of others to fail in any school task.

It is interesting to note that the terms **cooperation** and **competition** are antonymous; therefore, the reconciliation of children's competitive needs and cooperative needs is not an easy matter. In a sense we are confronted with an ambivalent condition that, if not carefully handled, could place children in a state of conflict, thus causing them to suffer distress.

This was recognized by Horney[12] over a half century ago when she indicated that on the one hand everything is done to spur us toward success, which means that we must not only be assertive but aggressive, able to push others out of the way. On the other hand, we are deeply imbued with ideals which declare that it is selfish to want anything for

---

[11] J.N. Humphrey and J.H. Humphrey, Incidents in the school environment which induce stress in elementary school children (College Park, Maryland, 1977).

[12] K. Horney, *The Neurotic Personality of our Times* (New York, W.W. Norton and Co., Inc., 1937).

ourselves, that we should be humble, turn the other hand, be yielding. Thus, society not only rewards one kind of behavior (cooperation) but its direct opposite (competition). Perhaps more often than not our cultural demands sanction these rewards without provision of clear-cut standards of value with regard to specific conditions under which these forms of behavior might well be practiced. Thus, the child is placed in somewhat of a quandary as to when to compete and when to cooperate.

More recently, it has been found that competition does not necessarily lead to peak performance and may in fact interfere with achievement. In this connection, Kohn[13] reported on a survey on the effects of competition on sports, business and classroom achievement and found that 65 studies showed that cooperation promoted higher achievement than competition, 8 showed the reverse, and 36 showed no statistically significant difference. It was concluded that the trouble with competition is that it makes one person's success depend upon another's failure, and as a result when success depends on sharing resources, competition can get in the way.

In studying about competitive stress Scanlan and Passer[14] described this condition as occurring when a child feels (perceives) that he or she will not be able to perform adequately to the performance demands of competition. When the child feels this way, he or she experiences considerable threat to self-esteem which results in stress. They further described competitive stress as the negative emotion or anxiety that a child experiences when he or she perceived the competition to be personally threatening. Indeed, this is a condition that should not be allowed to prevail in the school environment.

Studying the problem objectively, Scanlan[15] used a sports environment to identify predictors of competitive stress. She investigated the influence and stability of individual differences and situational factors on the competitive stress experienced by 76 9- to 14-year-old wrestlers. The subjects represented 16 teams from one state and reflected a wide range of wrestling ability and experience. Stress was assessed by the children's form of the Competitive State Anxiety Inventory and was measured immediately before and after each of two consecutive tournament matches.

---

[13] A. Kohn, *No Contest: The Case Against Competition* (Boston, Houghton-Mifflin Co., 1986).

[14] T.K. Scanlan and M.W. Passer, *The Psychological and Social Affects of Competition* (Los Angeles, University of California, 1977).

[15] T.K. Scanlan, Social psychological aspects of competition for male youth sports participants: Predictors of competitive stress, *Journal of Sport Psychology* 6 (1984): 208-226.

The children's disposition, characteristic precompetition cognitions, perceptions of significant adult influences, psychological states, self-perceptions, and competitive outcomes were examined as predictors of prematch and postmatch anxiety in separate multiple regression analyses for each tournament Round. The most influential and stable predictors of prematch stress for both matches were competitive trait anxiety and personal performance expectancies, while win-loss and fun experienced during the match predicted postmatch stress for both rounds.

Prematch worries about failure and perceived parental pressure to participate were predictive of Round One prematch stress. Round One postmatch stress levels predicted stress after Round Two, suggesting some consistency in the children's stress responses. Sixty-one and 35 percent prematch and 41 and 32 percent of postmatch state anxiety variances was explained for Rounds One and Two, respectively.

THE STRESS OF CERTAIN SCHOOL SUBJECTS

There are various subject areas that could be considered as perennial nemeses for many students. Probably any subject could be stress inducing for certain students. Prominent among those subjects that have a reputation for being more stress inducing than others are those concerned with the **3 Rs.** For example, it has been reported that for many children, attending school daily and performing poorly is a source of considerable and prolonged stress. If the children overreact to environmental stresses in terms of increased muscle tension, this may interfere easily with the fluid muscular movement required in handwriting tasks, decreasing their performance and further increasing environmental stresses. Most educators have seen children squeeze their pencils tightly, press hard on their paper, purse their lips, and tighten their bodies, using an inordinate amount of energy and concentration to write while performing at a very low level.[16]

Reading is another area of school activity that is loaded with anxiety, stress, and frustration for many children. In fact, one of the levels of reading recognized by reading specialists is called the "frustration level." In terms of behavioral observations this can be described as the level in

---

[16] J.L. Carter and H.L. Russell, Relationship between reading frustration and muscle tension in children with reading disabilities, *American Journal of Clinical Feedback* 2 (1979): 2.

which children evidence tension, excessive or erratic body movements, nervousness, and distractibility. This frustration level is said to be a sign of emotional tension or stress with breakdowns in fluency and a significant increase in reading errors.

A study by Swain[17] was undertaken to determine the extent to which stress was a factor in primary school children's reading difficulties. She investigated referral and evaluation statements and diagnostic data from parents, teachers, reading specialists and counselors regarding signs of stress and potential stressors as factors in the reading difficulties of 77 primary school children referred for evaluation at the Pupil Appraisal Center (PAC) at North Texas State University between 1977 and 1984.

Situational analysis was employed to obtain a holistic view of each child's reading difficulties. The researcher collected data from documented files at PAC. Data analysis via a categorical coding system produced 39 stress-related categories, organized under broad headings of family and school environment, readiness for reading/learning, general stress reactions, and responses to stress when reading/learning becomes a problem.

The most significant signs of stress cited in this study were symptoms of anxiety and a marked tendency toward passivity and unassertiveness. Primary potential stressors also emerged. Intellectual and language deficits were noted, along with self-defeating behaviors, absence of self-motivating/self-control, and problems stemming from the home and school environment.

Support for findings in referral and evaluation statements was found in diagnostic data which included intelligence, reading, and projective tests. Some of the children had specific personal limitations that might have hindered reading. However, many were experiencing frustration from working at capacity and yet not meeting parental or teacher expectations. No child was found to be coping effectively with apparent adverse circumstances. Failure by many of these children to adapt successfully to stress in their personal lives could forecast chronic difficulty in reading when it, too, becomes a challenge for them.

The subject that appears to stress the greatest majority of students is mathematics. This condition prevails from the study of arithmetic upon entering school through the required courses in mathematics in college. This has become such a problem in recent years that there is now an

---

[17] C.J. Swain, "Stress as a factor in primary school children's reading difficulties" (Doctoral diss., North Texas State University, Denton, TX, 1985).

area of study called "math anxiety" that is receiving increasing attention. Prominent among those studying this phenomenon is Sheila Tobias,[18] some of whose findings are summarized in the following discussion.

There appears to be what could be called "math anxious" and "math avoiding" people who tend not to trust their problem-solving abilities and who experience a high level of stress when asked to use them. Even though these people are not necessarily "mathematically ignorant," they tend to feel that they are, simply because they cannot focus on the problem at hand or because they are unable to remember the appropriate formula. Thus, a feeling of frustration and incompetence are likely to make them reluctant to deal with mathematics in their daily lives. It is suggested that at the root of this self-doubt is a fear of making mistakes and appearing stupid in front of others.

It is believed that there are at least three sources of anxiety commonly found in traditional mathematics classes: (1) time pressure, (2) humiliation, and (3) emphasis on one right answer.

As far as time pressure is concerned, such things as flash cards, timed tests, and competition in which the object is to finish first are among the first experiences that can make lasting negative impressions, and slower learners are soon likely to become apprehensive when asked to perform a mathematics problem.

One of the strongest memories of some math-anxious adults is the feeling of humiliation when being called upon to perform in front of the class. The child may be asked to go to the chalkboard to struggle over a problem until a solution is found. If an error is made, the child may be prodded to locate and correct it. In this kind of stressful situation it is not surprising that the child is likely to experience "math block," which adds to his sense of humiliation and failure. This should not be interpreted to mean that the chalkboard should not be used creatively to demonstrate problem-solving abilities. A child who successfully performs a mathematical task in front of classmates can have the enjoyable experience of instructing others. Also, the rest of the class can gain useful information from watching how another solves a problem. When using chalkboard practice, however, it is important to remember that children profit from demonstrating their competence and not their weaknesses.

Although mathematics problems do, in most cases, have right answers, it can be a mistake to always focus attention on accuracy. In putting too much emphasis on the end product, oftentimes overlooked is

---

[18] Sheila Tobias, Stress in the math classroom, *Learning* January (1981).

the valuable information about the process involved in arriving at that product. It would be well for teachers to reward creative thinking as well as correct answers. Again, the reader should not interpret this as meaning that the right answer is not important. However, when it is emphasized to the exclusion of all other information, students can become fearful of making mistakes and possibly angry with themselves when they do.

TEST PHOBIA

In over 40 years as a teacher (which included all levels from elementary school through the university graduate level), I have observed many students who were seriously stressed by "test phobia," or what has now become more commonly known as **test anxiety.**

Well over two decades ago, The Society for Research in Child Development released two monographs that contained extensive longitudinal studies on test anxiety as it related to school children.[19]

The first study represented a limited attempt to determine the relation over time between anxiety and indices of intellectual and academic performance. The following three major results were revealed:

1. The expected negative correlation between test anxiety and IQ tends to be small and insignificant in the first year, but increases significantly in the negative direction over time.
2. These tendencies are more marked and significant when measures designed to correct for sources of distortion of self-report are used.
3. The strength of the negative correlations between test anxiety and IQ scores are consistently stronger when third grade rather than first grade test anxiety scores are used as the predictor variable.

The second study is the summation of a longitudinal study of defensiveness to intelligence and achievement test performance and of school progress over the elementary school years. Some of the major findings indicated the following:

1. There was an increasingly negative relationship between anxiety and test performance over the entire elementary school experience.
2. Anxiety was greater on verbal than on non-verbal tests.
3. Unfamiliar tests aroused much anxiety.

---

[19] K.T. Hill and S.B. Saransen, The relation of test anxiety and defensiveness to test and school performance over the elementary school years, *Monograph of The Society for Research in Child Development* 2 (1966): Serial No. 104.

In addition to the above reports, a great deal of research has appeared on test anxiety in various sources over the years. One literature review on the subject suggested the following generalization:[20]

1. A critical factor is what the test situation means to a particular individual in terms of his learned patterns of response to anxiety. If the test is considered important to the individual and if he is anxious when taking tests, he is more likely to perform poorly on tests than one who is less anxious.
2. There is a negative relationship between level of ability and level of anxiety. Poorer students tend to be most anxious when facing a test.
3. There is a positive correlation between level of anxiety and level of aspiration. Those who are least anxious when facing a test tend to be those who have the least need or desire to do well in it.
4. Extreme degrees of anxiety are likely to interfere with test performance; however, a mild degree of anxiety facilitates test performance.
5. The more familiar a student is with tests of a particular type, the less likely he is to suffer extreme anxiety.
6. Test anxiety can enhance learning if it is distributed at a relatively low level throughout a course of instruction rather than being concentrated at a relatively high level just prior to and during a test.
7. There are low-to-moderate negative relationships between measures of anxiety and performance on very complex tasks. This negative relationship tends to increase as the task becomes more test-like.
8. Test anxiety increases with grade level and appears to be long range rather than transitory.

In a more recent literature review, Tryon[21] found that a significant negative relationship has been established between test anxiety and grade-point average and between anxiety and various aptitude and achievement tests.

Brown and Rosenbaum[22] contend that perceived stress appears to depend on psychological sets and responses that individuals are more likely to bring into the testing situation than manufacture on the spot. Stu-

---

[20] C. Kirkland, The effect of tension on students and schools, *Review of Educational Research*, 41 (1971).

[21] G.S. Tryon, The measurement and treatment of test anxiety, *Review of Educational Research*, 50 (1980): 343-372.

[22] B. Brown and L. Rosenbaum, Stress and competence, chap. 7 in *Stress in Childhood*, ed. J.H. Humphrey (New York, AMS Press, Inc., 1984), pp. 127-154.

dents respond to tests and testing situations with learned patterns of stress reactivity. The patterns may vary among individuals and may reflect differences in autonomic nervous system conditioning, feelings of threat or worry regarding the symbolic meaning of the test or the testing situation, and coping skills that govern the management of complexity, frustration, information load, symbolic manipulation, and mobilization of resources. There are also individual patterns of maladaptive behavior such as anxiety, a sustained high level of autonomic activity after exposure to a stressor and the use of a variety of such defense mechanisms as learned helplessness and avoidance behavior.

Perceived stress also depends upon the nature of the task to be performed. As tasks get more complex and require greater degrees of coordination and integration of the nervous system, a given stressor level will affect task performance as if it were a stronger stressor.

What then does the nature of test anxiety imply for educational goals and practices? Perhaps there should be a continuing opportunity for all school personnel and parents to report on their experiences with the tests that have been used. This feedback should also place a great deal of emphasis on the students' reactions to their testing experience. It is essential that the reactions of children that give evidence to emotional disturbance in relation to tests be carefully considered, especially when test results are interpreted and used for instructional, guidance and administrative purposes.

Finally, it is important to take a positive attitude when considering test results. That is, emphasis should be placed on the number of answers that were correct. For example, the child will more likely be encouraged if you say, "You got seven right," rather than "You missed three." There is evidence to show that this approach can help minimize stress in future test taking.

In closing this section of the chapter, mention should be made of the fact that it has long been known that stress can be induced upon children whose teachers themselves are under stress. This has been a problem for many years, and as long as three decades ago, on the basis of minimum incidence statistics and pupil-teacher ratios, it was estimated that anxiety may affect as many as 200,000 teachers and through them 5,000,000 students may be affected.[23]

---

[23] C. Kaplan, *Mental Health and Human Relations* (New York, Harper and Row, 1959).

PROGRAMS TO RELIEVE SCHOOL STRESS

In addition to an out-of-school life-style that is designed to minimize stress, it is important to develop in-school measures such as relaxation programs to reduce stressfulness in the daily school lives of children. In this regard, some attempts have been made to provide such programs, using certain kinds of interventions to reduce stress for children in the school environment.

It would be very difficult, if not impossible, to identify the specific time when an effort was first made to provide for stress management and relaxation of school children. However, it could have occurred as a forerunner of what has now become commonly known as "recess" in most elementary schools. As far back as the early nineteenth century attempts were being made to provide for some sort of relief of mental tension in the school day. Perhaps the pioneer in this effort was the famous Swiss educator, Johann Henrich Pestalozzi (1746-1827).[24] While observing his own child, Pestalozzi noticed that after playing for a time the boy tended to concentrate on his studies for longer periods of time. Later, in 1895, Holmes[25] submitted research that indicated that the interjection of a short period of physical activity served to stimulate the mental performance that followed. As mentioned, these discoveries could no doubt have led to the innovation of recess — a 10- to 20-minute respite in the school day — which has been a tradition in most schools for many decades. Although this practice is not ordinarily thought of as a stress management program for children, it has been postulated that it has satisfactorily served the purpose of mental diversion from prolonged "mental fatigue." In recent years, more sophisticated approaches have been undertaken (and in some instances researched) to provide relief of tension for children in school. Some of these are considered in the following discussion.

In considering the school as a stress reduction agency, Sylwester[26] has discussed stress as an inappropriate overresponse to the kind of problems that occur in school. He feels that a school can function as a stress reduction agency when it provides students with the information and skills they need to solve the threatening problems they will confront in life and when it creates an environment that allows the staff to feel they are helping students.

---

[24] J.H. Humphrey, *Child Learning,* 2nd ed. (Dubuque, Iowa, 1974).

[25] Marion Holmes, The fatigue of the school hour, *Pedagogical Seminary,* 3 (1895): 62-69.

[26] Robert Sylwester, The school as a stress reduction agency, *Theory into Practice,* Winter, 22 (1983): 3-6.

In discussing school stress and anxiety interventions, Forman and O'Malley[27] believe that interventions aimed at management of school-related stress provide a viable means of delivery of school psychological services that have the potential for promoting the emotional and physical health of children and adults in school settings. They feel that schools are likely to be sources of stress because they provide a context in which performance and relationship demands are made. Behavioral and cognitive-behavioral stress management interventions for students and teachers are suggested that are directed at altering the individual's appraisal of the stressor and/or enhancing personal coping responses. These interventions include rational-emotive therapy, self-instructional training, and systematic desensitization. Implications for the practice of school psychology are considered and suggested directions for future research are presented.

Grant and Grant[28] have made recommendations on what school counselors should know about children under stress. They suggest that if counselors and helping professionals are to be successful in assisting children under stress, they must learn to appreciate the concept of individual differences and assist parents and educators in developing awareness and acceptance of these differences. Counselors must also develop outreach activities designed to identify and encourage children who lack the communication skills needed to express their desire for help. They submit the following suggestions that may be helpful in assisting children in developing the coping skills needed for survival:

1. Learn to recognize the early signs of excessive stress. Productive stress management requires identification.
2. Be positive and remain calm in counseling stressful youth. Children under stress often lack self-esteem.
3. Be sensitive to individual and cultural differences. No two children cope with anxiety the same way.
4. Pay attention to dramatic change in behavior. Frequent absenteeism, a sudden decrease in academic performance, increased illness, and disruptive behavior may be an indication that crisis is occurring.
5. Help children understand that they are not alone. Reach out and be available.

---

[27] Susan G. Forman and Patricia L. O'Malley, School stress and anxiety interventions, *School Psychology Review*, Winter 13 (1984): 162-170.

[28] Arthur F. Grant and Audrey Grant, Children under stress: What every school counselor should know, *Journal of Non-White Concerns in Personnel and Guidance*, 11 (1982): 17-23.

6. Encourage children to communicate what they feel. Group counseling, home visits, role play, games and drawings may provide methods of establishing rapport.

Conger[29] conducted a study concerned with the effects of an anxiety-reducing program on anxiety levels of elementary school children. The purpose of this study was to determine the effectiveness of an anxiety-reducing program on anxiety levels as measured by the State-Trait Anxiety Inventory for Children (STAIC) for elementary students. The subjects (N = 80) in this study were male and female fourth grade students in Unified School District 257 in Iola, Kansas.

This study called for a two (treatment level) × two (subject sex) experimental design. The STAIC was given as a pretest and posttest to all subjects. A Digit Recall Task was administered to all subjects at the end of the study. The experimental group experienced the anxiety-reducing program. This program involved progressive muscle relaxation, imagery, role playing, and goal setting.

To determine if there were significant differences between the control vs. experimental or males vs. females, an analysis of variance was utilized. The statistical analysis revealed a significant difference between the two groups on the poststate anxiety scores. There was a significant difference between the experimental and control group on the Digit-Recall Task. There was a significant difference for sex on the post-trait anxiety scores, with females having a higher mean. There was no significant interaction for sex by group.

A two (treatment level) × two (anxiety level) ANOVA determined that there were significant differences between treatment groups and between low and high anxiety level subjects and an interaction of groups by anxiety level on the post-state (STAIC) scores. There was a significant difference between groups (treatment level) and between low and high anxiety level subjects on the post-trait scores. There was no interaction of group by anxiety level.

The results of this study indicated that this anxiety-reducing program did help the experimental group members to lower their state anxiety scores and achieve higher digit-recall scores. Those with high anxiety levels tended to be more successful in lowering their scores.

---

[29] Catherine D. Conger, "The effects of an anxiety reducing program on anxiety levels of elementary school children" (Doctoral diss., Kansas State University, Manhattan, KS, 1985).

In a similar study, Hutchison[30] examined the effectiveness and feasibility of a stress management program for third grade children. She mentions that to ameliorate the negative effects of anxiety on learning in the school setting, anxiety management programs have been developed and utilized with positive results with special needs students under special conditions. Since all school children are potential victims of negative effects of anxiety, a systematic investigation of the effectiveness and the feasibility of a stress management program in the regular classroom and instructed by the classroom teacher was deemed important.

From volunteers, three third grade teachers and their students were selected to participate in this investigation. Two of the teachers were assigned to teach the Stress Management Program, a six-week program of daily lessons which involved skill training in muscular relaxation, breathing techniques, guided fantasy, self-talk, tension awareness, structured reinforcement, generalization, and maintenance activities. The third teacher was assigned to use the placebo treatment Break-Time, a program emphasizing divergent processing activities.

The dependent variables included: ability to relax, teacher ratings of achievement-related behaviors, student's self-report of anxiety, generalization of relaxation skills, and attitudes of teachers and children toward the program. The independent variables were class membership and special education services membership. The changes on the dependent variables were measured from pre- to post-test, and on some variables, to follow-up. A multivariate analysis of variance revealed significant differences by class membership and no significant interaction between class membership and special education services membership. A multiple discriminant analysis indicated that membership in the treatment classes could be best predicted by decreases in external behavior and externally reliant behavior, both related to poor academic achievement.

The other major findings relating to the problem were that the trained students generalized the use of their relaxation-related skills, and both students and teachers held a positive attitude toward the program. The conclusion was that a stress-management program is both feasible and effective when taught by the classroom teacher in a regular classroom, assuming a teacher who is convinced of the importance of the program and who is willing to allow adequate class time for the learning, maintenance, and reinforcement of the skills.

---

[30] Susan Mordini Hutchison, "Effectiveness and feasibility of a stress management program for third grade children," (Doctoral diss., University of Illinois, Urbana-Champaign, IL, 1983).

From the preceding discussion it can be seen that stress reduction programs for children through relaxation have met with various degrees of success. Enough so at least to suggest that continued experimentation with them is indeed warranted.

These first three chapters have attempted to provide the reader with information about child development, childhood emotions and stress in the school environment. In the remainder of the book, we turn our attention to various forms of relaxation for children and how these can be successfully implemented in the school program.

Chapter 4

RELAXATION

LEARNING TO relax as a child could be as important to life in the future as many other lessons learned in school. Indeed, most teachers and children need some sort of relaxation to relieve the tensions encountered during the school day.

THE MEANING OF RELAXATION
AND RELATED TERMS

One derivation of the term **relax** is from the Latin word **relaxare**, meaning "loosen." It is interesting that a rather common parting comment among some people is the admonishment to "stay loose"—no doubt good advice.

The reality of muscle fibers is that they have a response repertoire of one. All they can do is contract, and this is the response they make to the electrochemical stimulation of impulses carried via the motor nerves. **Relaxation** is the removal of this stimulation.[1]

A relatively new term, **relaxation response** has been coined by Herbert Benson.[2] This involves a number of bodily changes that occur in the organism when one experiences deep muscle relaxation. There is a response against "overstress," which brings on these bodily changes and brings the body back into what is a healthier balance. Thus, the purpose of any kind of relaxation technique should be to induce a relaxation response.

---

[1] Barbara B. Brown, *Stress and the Art of Biofeedback* (New York, Bantam Books, Inc., 1978), p. 31.

[2] Herbert Benson, *The Relaxation Response* (New York, William Morrow and Company, Inc.), 1975.

It should be mentioned here that subsequent chapters will take into account the stress-reduction techniques of **meditation** and **biofeed-back**, both of which can indeed be considered as relaxation techniques. Therefore, it seems important at this point to give some attention to the theory underlying these techniques, all of which are concerned with mind-body interactions and all of which are designed to induce the relaxation response. In deep muscle **relaxation**, it is theorized that if the muscles of the body are relaxed, the mind in turn will be quieted. Theory involved in **meditation** is that if the mind is quieted, then other systems of the body will tend to be more readily stabilized. In the practice of **biofeedback**, the theoretical basis tends to involve some sort of integration of deep muscle relaxation and meditation. It is believed that the brain has the potential for voluntary control over all the systems it monitors and is affected by all of these systems. Thus, it is the intimacy of interaction between mind and body that has provided the mechanism through which one can learn voluntary control over biological activity.[3]

From the point of view of the physiologist, relaxation is sometimes considered as "zero activity" or as nearly zero as one can manage in the neuromuscular system. That is, it is a neuromuscular accomplishment that results in reduction, or possible complete absence of, muscle tone in a part of or in the entire body. It has been suggested that a primary value of relaxation lies in the lowering of brain and spinal cord activity, resulting from a reduction of nerve impulses arising in muscle spindles and other sense endings in muscles, tendons and joint structures.

The terms **relaxation, refreshment**, and **recreation** are often confused in their meaning. Although all of these factors are important to the well-being of the human organism, they should not be used interchangeably to mean the same thing. **Refreshment** is the result of an improved blood supply to the brain for "refreshment" from central fatigue and to the muscles for the disposition of their waste products. This explains in part why muscular activity is good for overcoming the fatigue of sitting quietly (seventh-inning stretch) and for hastening recovery after strenuous exercise (an athlete continuing running for a short distance slowly after a race).

Recreation may be described as the experience from which a person emerges with the feeling of being "re-created." No single activity is sure to bring this experience to all members of the group, nor is there assur-

---

[3] Richard A. Yarian, Relaxation techniques and relaxation response (Washington, DC, AAHPERD *Research Consortium Papers*, Vol. 1, Book 2, 1978).

ance that an activity will provide recreation again for a given person because it did so the last time. These are more the marks of a psychological than a physiological experience. An important essential requirement for a recreational activity is that it completely engross the individual; that is, it must engage his or her entire individual attention. It is really escape from the disintegrating effects of distraction to the healing effect of totally integrated activity. Experiences that produce this effect may range from a hard game of tennis to the reading of a comic strip.[4]

Some individuals consider recreation and relaxation to be one and the same thing, which is not the case. Recreation can be considered a type of mental diversion that can be helpful in relieving tension. Although mental and muscular tensions are interrelated, it is in the muscle that the tension state is manifested. For this reason, it appears important at this point to give a rather detailed explanation of the meaning of **tension**.

It is interesting to examine the entries for the terms stress and tension in the *Education Index*. This bibliographical index of periodical educational literature records entries on these terms as follows:

> **Stress** (physiology)
> **Stress** (psychology) see **Tension** (psychology)
> **Tension** (physiology) see **Stress** (physiology)
> **Tension** (psychology)

This indicates that there are physiological and psychological aspects of both stress and tension. However, articles in the periodical literature listed as "stress" articles seem to imply that stress is more physiologically oriented and that tension is more psychologically oriented. Thus, psychological stress and psychological tension could be interpreted to mean the same thing. The breakdown in this position is seen where there is another entry for tension concerned with **muscular** tension. The latter, of course, must be considered to have a physiological orientation. In the final analysis, the validity of these entries will depend upon the point of view of each individual. As will be seen later, the validity of this particular cataloging of these terms may possibly be at odds with a more specific meaning of the term.

The late Arthur Steinhaus,[5] a notable physiologist, considered tensions as unnecessary or exaggerated muscle contractions, which could be accompanied by abnormally great or reduced activities of the internal

---

[4] Arthur Steinhaus, *Toward an Understanding of Health and Physical Education* (Dubuque, IA, Wm. C. Brown Publishers, 1963), p. 73.

[5] Arthur Steinhaus, *Toward an Understanding of Health and Physical Education* (Dubuque, IA, Wm. C. Brown Publishers, 1963), p. 75.

organs. He viewed tensions in two frames of reference: first, as **phy-siologic** or **unlearned tensions**, and second, as **psychologic** or **learned** tensions. An example of the first, physiologic or unlearned tensions, would be "tensing" at bright lights or intense sounds. He considered psychologic or learned tension responses to stimuli that ordinarily do not involve muscular contractions, but that at sometime earlier in a person's experience were associated with a situation in which tension was a part of the normal response. In view of the fact that the brain connects any events that stimulate it simultaneously, it would appear to follow that, depending upon the unlimited kinds of personal experiences one might have, he may show tension to any and all kinds of stimuli. An example of a psychologic or learned tension would be an inability to relax when riding in a car after experiencing or imagining too many automobile accidents.

In a sense, it may be inferred that physiologic or unlearned tensions are current and spontaneous, while psychologic or learned tensions may be latent as a result of a previous experience and may emerge at a later time. Although there may be a hairline distinction in the minds of some people, perhaps an essential difference between stress and tension is that the former is a physical and/or mental state concerned with wear and tear on the organism, while the latter is either a spontaneous or latent condition that can bring about this wear and tear.

For many years, recommendations have been made with regard to procedures individuals might apply in an effort to relax. In consideration of any technique designed to accomplish relaxation, one very important factor that needs to be taken into account is that learning to relax is a skill. That is, it is a skill based on the kinesthetic awareness of feelings of **tonus** (the normal degree of contraction present in most muscles, which keeps them always ready to function when needed). Unfortunately, it is a skill that very few of us practice — probably because we have little awareness of how to go about it.

One of the first steps in learning to relax is to experience tension. That is, one should be sensitive to tensions that exist in his or her body. This can be accomplished by voluntarily contracting a given muscle group, first very strongly and then less and less. Emphasis should be placed on detecting the signal of tension as the first step in "letting go" (relaxing).

You might wish to try the traditional experiment used to demonstrate this phenomenon. Raise one arm so that the palm of the hand is facing outward away from your face. Now, bend the wrist backward and try to point the fingers back toward your face and down toward the forearm. You should feel some **strain** at the wrist joint. You should also feel something else in the muscle and this is tension, which is due to the muscle contracting the hand backward. Now, flop the hand forward with the fingers pointing downward and you will have accomplished a **tension-relaxation** cycle.

As in the case of any muscular skill, learning how to relax takes time and one should not expect to achieve complete satisfaction immediately. After one has identified a relaxation technique that he or she feels comfortable with, increased practice should eventually achieve satisfactory results.

PROGRESSIVE RELAXATION

So that the reader will have an understanding of how to progressively relax the various muscle groups, this technique is discussed here. The technique developed by Edmund Jacobson many years ago is still the one most often referred to in the literature and probably the one that has had the most widespread application. In this technique, the person concentrates on progressively relaxing one muscle group after another. The technique is based on the procedure of comparing the difference between tension and relaxation. That is, as previously mentioned, one senses the feeling of tension in order to get the feeling of relaxation. In suggesting the use of the technique with children, Jacobson[6] indicates that for them, instructions in how to recognize the experience of contraction in various muscles may be to a large extent omitted.

As mentioned previously, learning to relax is a skill that you can develop in applying the principles of progressive relaxation. One of the first steps is to be able to identify the various muscle groups and how to tense them so that tension and relaxation can be experienced. However, before making suggestions on how to tense and relax the various muscle groups, there are certain preliminary measures that need to be taken into account:

1. You must understand that this procedure takes time and, like anything else, the more you practice the more proficient you should become with the skills.

---

[6] Edmund Jacobson, *You Must Relax,* 4th ed. (New York, McGraw-Hill Book Company, Inc., 1962), p. 147.

2. The particular time of day is important and this is pretty much an individual matter. Some recommendations suggest that progressive relaxation be practiced daily — sometime during the day and again in the evening before retiring. For many people this would be difficult unless one time period was set aside before going to school in the morning. This might be a good possibility and might help a person to start the day relaxed.

3. It is important to find a suitable place to practice the tensing-relaxing activities. Again, this is an individual matter, with some preferring a couch and others a comfortable chair.

4. Consideration should be given to the amount of time a given muscle is tensed. You should be sure that you are able to feel the difference between tension and relaxation. This means that tension should be maintained from about four to not more than eight seconds.

5. Breathing is an important concomitant in tensing and relaxing muscles. To begin with, it is suggested that three or more deep breaths be taken and held for about five seconds. This will tend to make for better rhythm in breathing. Controlled breathing makes it easier to relax and it is most effective when it is done deeply and slowly. It is ordinarily recommended that one should inhale deeply when the muscles are tensed and exhale slowly when "letting go."

How to Tense and Relax Various Muscles

Muscle groups may be identified in different ways. The classification given here consists of four different groups: (1) muscles of the head, face, tongue, and neck, (2) muscles of the trunk, (3) muscles of the upper extremities, and (4) muscles of the lower extremities.

Muscles of the Head, Face, Tongue and Neck

There are two chief muscles of the head, the one covering the back of the head and the one covering the front of the skull. There are about 30 muscles of the face, including muscles of the orbit and eyelids, mastication, lips, tongue, and neck. Incidentally, it has been estimated that it takes 26 facial muscles to frown and a proportionately much smaller number to smile.

Muscles in this group may be tensed and relaxed as follows (relaxation is accomplished by "letting go" after tensing):

1. Raise the eyebrows by opening the eyes as wide as possible. You might wish to look into a mirror to see if you have formed wrinkles on the forehead.

2. Tense the muscles on either side of the nose like you were going to sneeze.
3. Dilate or flare out the nostrils.
4. Force an extended smile from "ear to ear" at the same time clenching your teeth.
5. Pull one corner of your mouth up and then the other up as in a "villainous sneer."
6. Draw your chin up as close to your chest as possible.
7. Do the opposite of the above, trying to draw your head back as close to your back as possible.

Muscles of the Trunk

Included in this group are the muscles of the back, chest, abdomen, and pelvis. Here are some ways you can tense some of these muscles.

1. Bring your chest forward and at the same time put your shoulders back with emphasis on bringing your shoulder blades as close together as possible.
2. Try to round your shoulders and bring your shoulder blades far apart. This is pretty much the opposite of the above.
3. Give your shoulders a shrug, trying to bring them up to your ears at the same time as you try to bring your neck downward.
4. Breathe deeply and hold it momentarily and then blow out the air from your lungs rapidly.
5. Draw in your stomach so that your chest is out beyond your stomach. Exert your stomach muscles by forcing out to make it look like you are fatter than you are.

Muscles of the Upper Extremities

This group includes muscles of the hands, forearms, upper arms, and shoulders. A number of muscles situated in the trunk may be grouped with the muscles of the upper extremities, their function being to attach the upper limbs to the trunk and move the shoulders and arms. In view of this, there is some overlapping in muscle groups **two** and **three**. Following are some ways to tense some of these muscles.

1. Clench the fist and then open the hand, extending the fingers as far as possible.
2. Raise one arm shoulder high and parallel to the floor. Bend at the elbow and bring the hand in toward the shoulder. Try to touch your shoulders while attempting to move the shoulder away from the hand. Flex your opposite biceps in the same manner.

3. Stretch one arm out to the side of the body and try to point the fingers backward toward the body. Do the same with the other arm.
4. Hold the arm out the same way as above, but this time have the palm facing up and point the fingers inward toward the body. Do the same with the other arm.
5. Stretch one arm out to the side, clench the fist and roll the wrist around slowly. Do the same with the other arm.

Muscles of the Lower Extremities

This group includes muscles of the hips, thighs, legs, feet, and buttocks. Following are ways to tense some of these muscles.

1. Hold one leg out straight and point the toes as far forward as you can. Do the same with the other leg.
2. Do the same as above but point the toes as far backward as you can.
3. Turn each foot outward as far as you can and release. Do just the opposite by turning the foot inward as far as you can.
4. Try to draw the thigh muscles up so that you can see the form of the muscles.
5. Make your buttocks tense by pushing down if you are sitting in a chair. If you are lying down try to draw the muscles of the buttocks in close by attempting to force the cheeks together.

The above suggestions include several possibilities for tensing various muscles of the body. As you practice some of these, you will also discover other ways to tense and then let go. A word of caution might be that, in the early stages, you should be alert to the possibility of cramping certain muscles. This can happen particularly with those muscles that are not frequently used. This means that at the beginning you should proceed carefully. It might be a good idea to keep a record or diary of your sessions so that you can refer back to these experiences if this might be necessary. This will also help you to get into each new session by reviewing your experiences in previous sessions.

USING RELAXATION WITH CHILDREN

According to Armstrong, Collins and Walker,[7] clinical experience and empirical research with adults suggest that relaxation training

---

[7] F.D. Armstrong, F.L. Collins, and C.E. Walker, Relaxation training with children: A review of the literature, in *Human Stress: Current Selected Research, Vol. 2,* ed. J.H. Humphrey (New York, AMS Press, Inc., 1988), pp. 201-233.

might be an effective intervention for reducing and possibly preventing stress-related problems in children. However, such research evaluating the effectiveness of relaxation with children has only begun appearing with regularity in the past 10 years. They assert that the need for an evaluation of relaxation training with children is clear, particularly with increased prescription of relaxation as an intervention for a variety of child problems ranging from hyperactivity to asthma.

After reviewing some 30 studies, they suggest that the results clearly support the labeling of relaxation training as the "aspirin" of behavior therapy for children as well as for adults. They found that relaxation training has been applied to numerous topographically and functionally different problems and in all cases had enhanced performance, had reduced behavioral distress, or had no effect at all. It has never been found to be harmful.

Progressive Relaxation for Children

The relaxation techniques used with children follow the same theory of relaxation used with adults; that is, the purpose is to experience tension in a muscle or group of muscles and then "let go."

Some attempts have been made to modify Jacobson's progressive relaxation technique for children. Notable in this regard is the prominent California psychologist, Stewart Bedford,[8] who has made the following recommendations in his book for children:

1. Find a comfortable place to relax. You can do it lying down or on a bed or the floor. You can do it in a recliner or sitting in a chair. If you practice relaxing in different positions, it will be easier for you to transfer this training into your life in general. After you have learned to relax, you will probably want to relax in more than one way and in more than one place. If you relax sitting down, it will be easier to relax while sitting at your desk. If you relax while lying down, it will be easier to go to sleep when you want to.

2. Don't wear shoes or tight clothes. It's best to be warm but not too hot.

3. When you get yourself into a comfortable position, take a deep breath. Fill your lungs with air while you count slowly to ten. Then let the air out—all out. Concentrate on how your lungs feel when they are full of air and how they feel when they are empty.

---

[8] Stewart Bedford, *Stress and Tiger Juice* (Chico, CA, Scott Publications, 1980), pp. 43-45.

4. Now think about your hands. Tense the muscles in your hands. Make fists. Think about how your hands feel when they are tense. Hold the tension while you count slowly to ten. Now relax the muscles in your hands and think about how they feel when they are relaxed. Concentrate on how your hands feel.

5. Now tense the muscles in your shoulders and arms. Think about how these muscles feel when they are tense. Hold this tension while you count slowly to ten. Now relax and think about how the muscles feel when they are relaxed. Get acquainted with your tense feelings. Get acquainted with your relaxed feelings. Learn how your body feels.

6. Now tense the muscles in your forehead. Raise your eyebrows as high as you can and think about how your face feels (think about how your face **feels**, not how it looks). Count slowly to ten and then relax. Now think about how these muscles feel when they are relaxed. Remember, think about the muscles when they are tense and when they are relaxed.

7. Now tense the muscles of your jaws. Clamp your teeth together and concentrate on how the muscles feel. Count slowly to ten and then relax. Now think about the muscles of your jaws when they are relaxed.

8. Take another deep breath. Hold the air in while you count slowly to ten. Think about your chest. Let the air out slowly and relax. Think about your chest when it is relaxed.

9. Arch your back a little and tense your back muscles. Hold the tension and think about it while you count slowly to ten. Now relax and think about the back muscles when they are relaxed.

10. Tighten the muscles of your stomach. Pretend that someone is going to sock you with a ball and you are going to brace yourself so it doesn't hurt. Concentrate on the tight muscles. Count slowly to ten. Relax. Think about the muscles in your stomach when they are relaxed.

11. Tense the muscles in both legs and both feet. Hold the tension while you count slowly to ten. Think about the muscles when they are tense. Relax. Now think about the muscles when they are relaxed.

12. Now, try to relax all the muscles in your body. Get as comfortable as you can. Concentrate on your beathing. Think about the air coming into your body and going out of your body. Air coming in. Air going out. Concentrate on your breathing. Breathe deeply. Breathe slowly. Practice letting your stomach muscles pull the air in and

push the air out. Concentrate on this and do this kind of breathing for about five minutes. If you start thinking about other ideas, pull your thoughts back to your breathing. Air coming in. Air going out. Air coming in. Air going out.

13. If you go to sleep while doing this part of the exercise, don't worry. If you stay awake, you will get more good out of the relaxation, but a little sleep doesn't hurt us now and then. If you do these activities twice a day, you will gradually learn how to get into deep muscle relaxation. When you have learned to control relaxation in your muscles, you have learned one of the methods of managing your stress energies. You have learned a little more about the control of your emergency reaction. Remember, it is hard to be tense and relaxed at the same time.

Others have used versions of progressive relaxation with children. For example, two of my collaborators on a childhood stress project, psychologists John Carter and Harold Russell,[9] have developed a series of tapes for child relaxation. One of these is patterned after the idea of progressive relaxation and involves tensing and relaxing various muscle groups. This is to help make the children aware of their own muscular tension and to learn how it feels to release their tensions. In the following sequence children are asked to tense for five seconds and then to relax and feel the tension leaving for ten seconds.

1. Squeeze your eyes shut — tightly — hold it, relax.
2. Push your lips together, very tightly — hold it, relax.
3. Press your tongue to the roof of your mouth — hold it, relax.
4. Shrug your shoulders up toward your ears — hold it — relax — feel the tension leaving.
5. With both hands make a fist as tight as you can — feel the tension building — relax. Feel the tension leaving.
6. Make a fist with your right hand. Notice the difference between your tense right hand and your relaxed left. Relax your right hand.
7. Make a fist with your left hand. Feel the left hand getting tense while your right hand is relaxing — relax your left hand.
8. Pull your stomach way in toward your backbone — hold it — relax — feel the tension leaving.
9. Push your knees together — hard — hold it. Relax.

---

[9] John L. Carter and Harold Russell, Use of biofeedback relaxation procedures with learning disabled children, in *Stress in Childhood*, ed. J.H. Humphrey (New York, AMS Press, Inc., 1984), p. 286.

10. Pull your toes toward your knees, way up. Hold it, hold it, relax. Feel the tension leaving your legs.
11. Point your toes. Hold it — relax.
12. Now tighten every muscle in your body — hold it — relax your entire body. Let your entire body get very limp — relaxed and comfortable.

When this is completed, breathing instructions are presented. The children are asked to breathe in through their nose and out through their mouth. They are asked to do this naturally and rhythmically. Each time they breathe out, they are reminded to let themselves get just a little more limp, a little more relaxed, and a little more comfortable.

Finally, Harry Krampf[10] and his associates report success with what they call **guided progressive sessions** as a part of a Summer Youth Fitness School for children ages 7 to 14. They used a series of guided progressive sessions to assist the participants in becoming aware of their tensions and how to release these tensions. In this format, there are four component parts: (1) relaxation of individual muscles, (2) relaxation of groups of muscles, (3) relaxation of principal muscle groups, and (4) relaxation of the total body. It is suggested that the practice setting be conducive to relaxation, and this includes a comfortable room temperature, loose-fitting clothing, lighting that is not too bright, and the provision of a soft surface such as mats. The first step involves practice of controlled breathing followed by helping children to realize the difference between being tense and limp. The next step is to use the tensing-releasing procedure, progressing through the various body parts.

---

[10] Harry Krampf, Dave Hopkins, and John Bird, Muscular relaxation for the elementary school student, *Journal of Physical Education and Recreation* April (1979).

Chapter 5

FORMAL CLASSROOM
RELAXATION EXERCISES

THE WORD **formal** as used here refers to specifically named exercises that are conducted in a more or less formalized manner. In contrast, relaxation activities recommended in subsequent chapters are those that are performed under more subtle conditions.

When used in connection with the human organism, the term **physical** means a concern for the body and its needs. The term **activity** derives from the word **active**, one meaning of which is the requirement of action. Thus, when the two words physical and activity are used together, it implies body action. This is a broad term and could include any voluntary and/or involuntary body movement. When such body movement is practiced for the purpose of developing and maintaining physical fitness, it is ordinarily referred to as physical **exercise**.[1]

IMPORTANCE OF EXERCISE IN
REDUCING STRESS AND TENSION

The value of exercise as a means of reducing stress and tension is well documented by various sources. According to Walter McQuade and Ann Aikman,[2] one of the many stresses people suffer from is stress resulting from their own pent-up aggressive drives. When people express these drives in physical action, they are better off because exercise not only dispels this form of stress, but also it enables the body to hold up better against stress in general.

---

[1] James H. Humphrey, *A Textbook of Stress* (Springfield, IL, Charles C Thomas, Publisher, 1982), p. 93.

[2] Walter McQuade and Ann Aikman, *Stress* (New York, E.P. Dutton and Co., Inc., 1974), p. 130.

71

Similarly, Beata Jencks[3] reports that physical and emotional trauma upset balance of body and mind, and that much energy is wasted in muscular tension, bringing on unnecessary tiredness and exhaustion. If stress reactions become habit patterns, then the muscles and tendons shorten and thicken and excessive connective tissue is deposited, causing a general consolidation of tissues. She comments further that excess energy, released by action of the sympathetic nervous system, if not immediately dissipated by muscular action, produces muscular or nervous tension and that this tension should be dissipated by muscular action in the form of exercise.

It has been suggested by C. Eugene Walker[4] that exercise is very effective in reducing anxiety, although he states that how this occurs is not entirely understood. It may be that it satisfies the evolutionary need of man to engage in large muscle, physically aggressive activity that was very adaptive for primitive man, but with our highly civilized, sedentary, and confined life-style had fewer acceptable outlets. He concludes that whatever the basis for it, exercise does have an anxiety- and tension-reducing effect. People on exercise programs tend to be more healthy, have better vital capacity, handle problems better, sleep better, and cope with life in general in a more satisfactory way. Over a period of time people on such programs generally feel better, are more optimistic, and have better self-images. Thus, exercise immediately reduces anxiety somewhat and over the long run tends to inoculate against the development of future anxieties.

As far as objective scientific inquiry is concerned, over a period of years a number of controlled studies have provided evidence that physical activity contributes to one's capacity to reduce stress. One representative example of such research is the work of Richard Driscoll.[5] He used forty minutes of stress treatment and a combination of physical exertion and positive imagery to determine their effect upon anxiety reduction. High-anxiety students were tested in six conditions, including one group that received standard systematic desensitization (to be discussed in a later chapter), one that received the exercise and imagery treatment, and a control group that received no treatment. After witnessing a sequence of stressful scenes, the group that was most successful

---

[3] Beata Jencks, *Your Body Biofeedback at Its Best* (Chicago, Nelson-Hall, Inc., 1977), pp. 51, 172.

[4] C. Eugene Walker, *Learn to Relax, 13 Ways to Reduce Tension* (Englewood Cliffs, NJ, Prentice-Hall, Inc., 1975), pp. 76-77.

[5] Richard Driscoll, Exertion therapy, *Behavior Today* VI (1975).

in effectively reducing anxiety was the one that used the physical exertion of running, plus positive imagery of themselves being calm and tranquil. It was found that the combination of positive imagery and physical exertion reduced the anxiety the most. This study is supportive of other evidence that suggests that stress reduction means simply giving one an acceptable way of recovering from a stressful incident.

TYPES OF EXERCISES

Generally speaking, the two best known types of exercise are **isotonic** and **isometric**.[6]

Isotonic Exercises

These are the types of exercises with which most people are familiar. An isotonic exercise involves the amount of resistance one can overcome during one application of force through the full range of motion in a given joint or joints. An example of this would be picking up a weight and flexing the elbows while lifting the weight, let us say, to shoulder height.

Isotonics can improve strength to some extent. They are also very useful for increasing and maintaining full range of motion. Such range of motion should be maintained throughout life if possible, although it can decrease with age and with such musculoskeletal disorders as arthritis. This disease can cause shortening of fibrous tissue structures and this is likely to limit the normal range of motion.

Another important feature of isotonic exercise is that it can increase circulatory-respiratory endurance in such activities as running (jogging) and swimming.

Isometric Exercises

Although isometrics do not provide much in the way of improvement of normal range of motion and endurance, they are most useful in increasing strength and volume of muscles. In isometrics the muscle is contracted, but the length of the muscle is generally the same during contraction as during relaxation. The contraction is accomplished by keeping two joints rigid while at the same time contracting the muscle(s)

---

[6] James H. Humphrey, Combat stress with exercise, *Total Health* January (1983):9.

between the joints. A maximal amount of force is applied against a fixed resistance during one all-out effort. An example of this is pushing or pulling against an immovable object. Let us say that if you place your hands against a wall and push with as much force as you can, you have effected the contraction of certain muscles while their length has remained essentially the same.

EXERCISES FOR STRESSFUL CLASSROOM SITUATIONS

As mentioned previously, many stressful conditions can prevail in the school environment. The present discussion is concerned with the child's active behavior in a stressful situation. More specifically, what exercises can teachers provide for children to help them deal with a stressful situation in the classroom?

Various authentic pronouncements have been made that support the idea that instant activity can be beneficial. For example, Reuven Gal and Richard Lazarus[7] report that being engaged in activity, rather than remaining passive, is preferable in most individuals in most stressful situations and can be highly effective in reducing threat and distress. Lazarus[8] has also maintained that a person may alter his or her psychological and physiological stress reactions in a given situation simply by taking action, and this, in turn, will affect his or her appraisal of the situation, thereby ultimately altering the stress reaction.

What then are some of the physical exercises that teachers can have children engage in as a reaction to a stressful situation? Obviously, it would not seem to be appropriate to engage in isotonics by dropping to the floor and start doing push-ups or to break into a jog around the room. Isometrics are recommended for this purpose and the following are some possibilities. Certainly, creative teachers will be able to think of others.

1. Hand and Head Press. Interweave fingers and place hands at the back of the head with elbows pointing out. Push the head backward on the hands while simultaneously pulling the head forward with the hands. This can be done while standing or sitting at a desk.

---

[7] Reuven Gal and Richard S. Lazarus, The role of activity in anticipating and confronting stressful situations, *Journal of Human Stress* December (1975).

[8] Richard S. Lazarus, The self-regulation of emotion, in *Parameters of Emotion*, ed. L. Levy (New York, Raven Press), 1975.

2. Wall Press. Stand with the back against the wall. Allow the arms to hang down at the sides. Turn hands toward the wall and press the wall with the palms, keeping the arms straight.

3. Hand Pull. Bend the right elbow and bring the right hand in with the palm up close to the front of the body. Put the left hand in the right hand. Try to curl the right arm upward while simultaneously resisting with the left hand. Repeat using the opposite pressure. This can be done while standing or sitting at a desk.

4. Hand Push. The hands are clasped with the palms together close to the chest with the elbows pointing out. Press the hands together firmly.

5. Leg Press. While sitting at a desk or table, cross the left ankle over the right ankle. The feet are on the floor and the legs are at about a right angle. Try to straighten the right leg while resisting with the left leg. Repeat with the right ankle over the left ankle.

6. The Gripper. Place one hand in the other and grip hard. Another variation is to grip an object. While standing, this could be the back of a chair or, while sitting, it could be the arms of a chair or the seat.

7. Chair Push. While sitting at a desk or table with the hands on the armrests of the chair, push down with the hands. The entire buttocks can be raised from the chair seat. One or both feet can be lifted off the floor, or both can remain in contact with the floor.

8. Hip Lifter. While sitting at a desk or table, lift one buttock after the other from the chair seat. Try to keep the head from moving. The hands can be placed at the sides of the chair seat for balance.

9. Heel and Toe. From a standing position, rise on the toes. Come back down on the heels while raising both the toes and the balls of the feet.

10. Fist Clencher. Clench fists and then open the hands, extending the fingers as far as possible.

This short list is comprised of representative examples of isometric exercises, and they are actually referred to by some as **stress exercises.** While it has been recommended that these types of exercises can be performed easily in the school environment, it is obvious that they can be performed elsewhere as well. Wherever they are performed, it might be well to observe the following recommendations of the President's Council on Physical Fitness.[9]

---

[9] *Adult Physical Fitness* (Washington, DC, U.S. Printing Office), 1976.

For each contraction, maintain tension for no more than eight seconds. Do little breathing during the contraction; breathe deeply between contractions. Start easily and do not apply maximum effort in the beginning. For the first three or four weeks, one should exert only about one-half of what is the maximum force. The first three or four seconds should be used to build up to this degree of force—and the remaining four or five seconds to hold it.

The isometric exercises recommended here have met with success with teachers who have had children perform them in a stressful school situation.

It seems most appropriate to conclude this chapter with a statement from my friend, the late Hans Selye, who is generally known as the "Father of Stress."

> Physical activity is an excellent way to relieve the pressures bearing on our minds and to equalize the wear and tear throughout the body, giving overworked parts a time to rest. Most people seek diversion intuitively for these reasons, just as an athlete may read for relaxation, the sedentary man may engage in sports for a change of pace. The rich executive, although he would not dream of relaxing by moving heavy furniture, may enjoy a regular workout at his club's gym. Furthermore, we must not forget that while exercising is beneficial in reducing stress, it also helps us combat the physical decay of aging—indeed, this is one of the reasons I used to race about the university on my bicycle each morning.[10]

---

[10] Hans Selye, Stress and physical activity, *Stress, The Official Journal of the International Institute of Stress and Its Affiliates* Summer (1981):4.

Chapter 6

RELAXATION GAMES AND STUNTS

GAMES NOT ONLY play a very important part in the school program but in society in general. The unique quality of games and their application to situations in everyday living have become a part of various colloquial expressions. In many instances, descriptive words and phrases from games have become part of daily vocabulary and appear frequently in news articles and other written material. These words and phrases are used to describe a situation that is so familiar in a game situation that they give a clear meaning to an event from real life.

Many of us have used, at one time or another, the expression "That's the way the ball bounces" to refer to a situation in which the outcome was not as desirable as was anticipated. Or, "That's par for the course," meaning that the difficulty was anticipated and the results were no better or no worse than expected. When we are "home free" we tend to refer to having gotten out of a tight situation, with results better than expected. The expression "the bases are loaded" describes a situation in which a critical point has been reached and there is much at stake on the next event or series of events. If you have "two strikes against you," you are operating at a grave disadvantage, and if someone "strikes out," he has failed.

The value of games as an important intellectual influence in the school program has been recognized for decades. For example, as far back as 1909, Bancroft[1] observed that as a child's perceptions are quickened, he sees more quickly that the ball is coming toward him and he is in danger of being tagged, or that it is his turn; he hears the footsteps behind him, or his name or number called; he feels the touch on the shoulder; or in innumerable other ways he is aroused to quick and direct recognition of, and response to, things that go on around him.

---

[1] Jessie H. Bancroft, *Games* (New York, The Macmillan Company), 1909.

The physiological value of games has often been extolled because of the vigorous physical nature of many games in which children participate. And in more recent years a great deal of credence has been put in the potentialities for modifying human behavior within a social frame of reference that many games tend to provide. For instance, it has been suggested that the game is probably the child's first social relationship with strangers and his first testing of self against others.

Stunts are activities that involve competing against one's self and natural forces. These activities are based upon the child's desire to test his ability in such a way that he attempts to better his own performance. Stunts are concerned predominantly with certain kinds of imitations and the performance of a variety of kinds of feats that utilize such abilities as balance, coordination, flexibility, agility, and strength. (Some stunts are closely related to games and are sometimes referred to as **stunt games**.)

A RELAXATION GAME FORMAT

An example of the successful use of the game format in providing for relaxation in children is one suggested by Robert McBrien.[2] He used this approach in the tensing-releasing phase with the game **Simon Says.** Each muscle group to be tensed is prefaced by "Simon Says," that is, "Simon says to close your eyes...Simon says to make your eyebrows touch your hair...Simon says to let go and feel your eyes relax." A five-second tensing of any muscle is followed by 15 seconds of releasing the muscle. The sequence for relaxing the muscles prefaced by "Simon Says" follows:

1. Head
   a. Try to make your eyebrows touch your hair.
   b. Squeeze your eyes shut.
   c. Wrinkle up your nose.
   d. Press your lips together.
   e. Press your tongue against the roof of your mouth.
2. Shoulders and back
   a. Lift your shoulders and try to touch your ears.
   b. Bring your shoulders back as far as they will go.
3. Hands and arms
   a. Make your fists as tight as you can.
   b. Show me your arm muscles.

---

[2] Robert J. McBrien, Using relaxation methods with first grade boys, *Elementary School Guidance and Counseling* February (1978).

4. Stomach — Make your stomach as hard as you can; pull it way in.
5. Upper legs
   a. Lift your legs and feet off the floor.
   b. Press your knees together.
6. Lower legs and feet
   a. Press your ankles together.
   b. Press your feet together.

Note: The game Simon Says is played as follows: One or more children face the person who plays Simon. Every time Simon says to do something, the children do it; however, if a command is given without the prefix "Simon says," the child or children remain motionless. For example, when the leader issues the command, "Simon says press your ankles together," this is done, but if the leader just says, "Press your knees together," the command is not executed.

GAME AND STUNT STORIES

It is very interesting to children when games or stunts are presented in the form of a story. Several such stories provided here in one way or another involve contrasting tensing-relaxing movements. The stories can be read to the children or, depending upon their ability level, the children can read the stories themselves.

The stories are written about some sort of game or stunt that children will enjoy performing. It will be noticed that the experience depicted in each story is not readily identifiable. In the following selections the story is presented first, and this is followed by a **description** of the activity depicted in the story and a **suggested application.**

FRANKY FROG JUMPS
Franky Frog sits.
He is ready.
He jumps.
Sit like Franky.
Jump like Franky.

Description

The activity depicted in this story is the **frog jump.** A child squats down on feet and hands. He elevates himself off the surface area by springing into the air from both feet and hands and landing on both feet and hands.

Application

Before the story is read, the children can be engaged in a discussion of frogs and how they move. The discussion can focus on how a frog sits and then suddenly takes a jump. Body tension occurs when the frog (child) is preparing to jump as well as during the jump. There is release of tension at the end of the jump.

> WILLIE WORM
> I move like Willie Worm.
> I move in front.
> I move in back.
> I move along.
> I will stop quickly.

Description

The activity in this story is **measuring worm.** A child lies down facing the surface area. He pushes up and places his weight on his hands and toes. The elbows are straight and the body is stiff. He brings the feet up close to the hands by walking along while the hands are kept in place. The feet are then kept in place, and he walks along on the hands until the body is extended again. He continues in this manner.

Application

Discussion starts with how a worm moves. The children are then asked how they might do this. They try to perform the activity under the guidance of the teacher. There is tension of the body as a child prepares to move like a worm. This continues as he moves like Willie Worm. The teacher can give a signal to stop quickly, and at this point there is release of the tensed muscles.

> JUMPING JACK
> I am a jumping jack.
> I jump way up.
> I come way down.
> I will jump up and down.

Description

In the **jumping jack** the child stoops down low in a crouched position. He exerts his energy by jumping up. He tries to land lightly on his feet and then falls to the surface area. (Most activities that require landing should be performed on a soft landing surface such as a carpet or matting.)

Application

There can be a discussion of how a Jack-in-the-box functions. The children can then try to do this. Tension occurs during preparation for the jump and during the jump.

CURLY CAT TAKES A WALK

Curly Cat is asleep.
Curly Cat opens his eyes.
Curly Cat takes a walk.
He walks with long steps.
He holds his head high.
He walks around.
Try to walk like Curly Cat.
Put your hands on the floor.
Walk all around like Curly Cat.

Description

In the **cat walk** the child walks along on his hands and feet while trying to maintain an arch in his back.

Application

The discussion can start by asking how many have a cat as a pet. This can be followed by asking if they have ever watched the cat while it was sleeping and what it did when it awakened. Tension occurs as the child assumes the position for the walk, and it also occurs during the walk. The teacher can suggest that the cat suddenly stop and lie down. It is at this point that the muscles relax.

GEORGE GIRAFFE

There is a tall animal in a far away land.
He has a long neck.
His name is George Giraffe.
You could look like him if you did this.
Place your arms high over your head.
Put your hands together.
Point them to the front.
This will be his neck and head.
Now walk like George Giraffe.
This is how.
Stand on your toes.
Walk with your legs straight.

Description

In the **giraffe walk** the child stands straight with his arms extended upward. The wrists are bent forward with the fingers pointing straight ahead. The thumbs can be interlocked. The child walks along with his legs stiff.

Application

The discussion can begin by asking children if they have ever been to a zoo. If some have had this experience, the discussion can focus upon the kinds of animals in the zoo. The teacher can guide the discussion so that attention is directed to a giraffe. If none of the children have been to a zoo, the teacher can ask if they have been to a circus or have seen a circus on television. It is also very useful to begin the discussion with a picture of a giraffe. In assuming the position for the giraffe walk and actually performing the walk, there is a great deal of muscle tension. As in the case of the previous activity (cat walk), the teacher may give a signal for the giraffe to drop to the surface area. This provides for muscular relaxation.

> THE JUMPING RABBIT
> I can jump like a rabbit.
> I will sit like a rabbit.
> I put my hands on the floor.
> Now I jump.
> My feet come up to my hands.
> I hold my hands in front.
> I put my hands on the floor.
> I jump again and again.
> On the last jump I will fall down.

Description

In the **rabbit jump** the child stoops to a squatting position. The hands are placed on the floor in front. A jump is made with both feet to bring them up close to the hands. The hands are then placed in front again. Several jumps are performed in this manner.

Application

The teacher can engage the children in any type of discussion that involves rabbits and their habits. In this discussion, consideration can be given regarding how rabbits move. There is tension in the preparation for the jump and the jump itself. There is relaxation when the rabbit falls over on the last jump.

THE GROWING FLOWERS
Flowers grow.
First they are seeds.
Be a seed.
Grow like a flower.
Grow and grow.
Keep growing.
Grow tall.
Now you are a flower.
Now, wilt like a flower.

Description

In this activity, a child acts out the growth of a flower; the starting position is one in which the child squats down low as close to the surface area as possible. He then stretches (grows) as tall as he can.

Application

A real flower or picture of a flower can be used in the discussion about flowers. The discussion can take into account the various kinds of flowers and what they need to make them grow and how they grow. Tension occurs during the growing period, and there is relaxation when the flower wilts.

FALLING LEAVES
Trees stand tall and straight.
Stand tall and straight like a tree.
Trees have leaves.
Leaves fall.
They fall from the trees.
They fall to the ground.
Fall like leaves.
Down, down, down.
Down to the ground.
Quiet leaves.
Rest like leaves.

Description

This is an activity in which the child dramatizes leaves falling from a tree. The child stands straight and stiff like a tree and then does movements that depict falling leaves.

Application

The activity can be introduced with any discussion about trees and their leaves. Tension occurs during the time the child stands stiff like a tree, and relaxation takes place as the child releases from the position and acts out the falling of leaves.

> MR. SNOWMAN AND MR. SUN
> See Mr. Snowman.
> Mr. Snowman is packed hard with snow.
> See Mr. Sun.
> Mr. Sun is Warm.
> Mr. Snowman sees Mr. Sun.
> Mr. Snowman is going.
> Going, going, going.
> Mr. Snowman is gone.
> Be Mr. Snowman.

Description

This activity is one in which a child dramatizes a melting snowman. In doing this, the child will give his idea of a snowman and what happens when the snowman melts.

Application

There are many ways to introduce this activity. One of the most effective ways is to discuss the building of a snowman and how long it will last. Reasons why a snowman melts can be discussed. The child's body is tense as he becomes a snowman of hard-packed snow. Relaxation occurs when he melts by being in the sun.

> CASPER CAMEL
> Casper Camel lives in the zoo.
> He has a hump on his back.
> Could you look like Casper Camel?
> You will need a hump.
> Try it this way.
> Bend forward.
> Put your arms behind your back.
> Hold them together.
> This will be a hump.
> That will look like Casper Camel.
> Take a step.
> Lift your head.
> Take a step.

Lift your head.
Move like Casper Camel.

Description

The activity depicted in this story is the **camel walk.** The child stands straight. The hands are placed behind the back and folded. Next, the child bends forward at the waist and tries to raise the arms in the back. The child walks along swinging from side to side.

Application

Before the story is read a discussion can focus on camels and how they walk. It might be a good idea to show a picture of a camel. Tension of the muscles of the trunk occurs when the child is preparing for the camel walk and when the movement is actually executed. After the child performs the activity for a short time, the teacher can give a call for the camel to fall and this action releases tension.

THE CLOWNS DO A STUNT
Have you ever seen clowns at a circus?
Sometimes they do funny things.
Once I saw two clowns do a stunt together.
This is what they did.
They sat back to back.
Their feet were flat on the floor.
Their feet were close to their bodies.
They locked their arms together.
They pushed their backs together.
They pushed hard.
As they pushed they began to rise.
At last they were standing.
They sat down and did the stunt again.
Could you do this stunt with a friend?

Description

This story is written about the stunt called **back-to-back get up.** It requires two children of about equal size. Success in performing the stunt depends upon each child pushing hard against the other to rise to the standing position.

Application

A discussion can be introduced about clowns and the many kinds of things they do to make people laugh. The story can then be read and the children can experiment with the stunt. A great deal of tension occurs when they are rising to the standing position, and it is relieved when they reach this position.

CIRCUS ELEPHANT
I saw the circus.
I saw many animals.
I saw an elephant.
He was big.
He had big legs.
He had a trunk.
He swings his trunk.
I will walk like the elephant.

Description

This is the story about the stunt called the **elephant walk.** The child bends forward at the waist with knees straight. The arms are held straight down in front with the hands clasped. The child walks along slowly without bending the knees, swinging the arms from side to side.

Application

The discussion can begin with circus elephants and how they move and what they do in the circus. There is tension in the muscles of the trunk as the child walks along with legs and arms stiff. To release the tension a signal can be given by the teacher for the elephant to fall down.

TICK, TOCK
Listen to the clock.
It says, "Tick, tock" as it keeps the time.
Would you like to play you are a clock?
This is the way.
Stand up.
Keep your arms straight.
Now keep time with the clock by moving your arms.
Ready.
Move your arms like a clock.
Keep your arms stiff and straight.
Here are some words to say to the "tick, tock" of the clock.
    Tick, tock, tick, tock.
    Be bright and gay.
    It's time to start another day.
    Tick, tock, tick, tock.
    Tick, tock, tick, tock.
    Oh! Oh! Let's stop the clock.

Description

In this activity the children pretend they are clocks. They use their arms as the hands of the clock. They move the arms as they say the verse.

Application

A discussion can begin about clocks and about why we need them. Children are asked to pretend to be a clock, and attention is focused on the hands of a clock. The arms are held very rigid as they move like the hands of a clock. When the clock stops, the arms are dropped and, thus, relaxed.

PUSH THE WHEELBARROW
Have you ever seen a wheelbarrow go?
You can play you are a wheelbarrow.
You will need a friend to play with you.
You can be the wheelbarrow.
You get down on your hands and knees.
Your hands will be the wheel.
You walk along on your hands.
Your friend steers the wheelbarrow.
Whoops! The wheelbarrow breaks down.
Now your friend can be the wheelbarrow.
You can steer the wheelbarrow.
Oh! Oh! The wheelbarrow breaks down again.

Description

The stunt depicted in this story is **the wheelbarrow.** A child has a partner of about equal size and strength. One child of the couple assumes a position with the hands on the floor with elbows straight and feet extended behind. The other child carries the feet of the first child, who keeps his knees straight. The child becomes a wheelbarrow by walking on his hands. Children change positions so that each can be the wheelbarrow.

Application

The discussion can begin about wheelbarrows, including what they are, how they run, and what can be done with them. Children are asked to think of ways that they could be a wheelbarrow. When the activity is performed, the child who is the wheelbarrow experiences a great deal of tension in the arms. There is relaxation when the wheelbarrow breaks down.

AIRPLANES GO
I look up.
I hold my arms out.

I am an airplane.
My arms are the wings.
They are stiff.
I go round and round.
I stop.

Description

In this activity the performer pretends to be an airplane, using the arms as the wings of the plane.

Application

Any discussion about airplanes is a lively one, and children like to pretend to be an airplane. Emphasis is placed on the importance of the wings and that they must be very strong. This tends to prompt the performer to hold the arms out very straight and stiff. Relaxation occurs when the airplane stops.

SIDNEY SEAL
Did you ever hear of a sea lion?
Sometimes he is called a seal.
He lives in the sea.
Sometimes he lives in the zoo.
There is one in the zoo called Sidney Seal.
He likes to swim.
He can also walk on land.
Would you like to try to walk like Sidney Seal?
Try it this way.
Put your hands on the floor.
Put your feet back.
Put your weight on your hands and on top of your toes.
Now walk on your hands and drag your legs.
Sidney Seal gets tired and falls down.

Description

The activity that is depicted in the story is the **seal walk.** The child moves along on the hands and drags the legs behind. The legs are held very rigid.

Application

The discussion can focus on seals, especially their habits and the different ways they can move. Many children will have seen them on television, if not in real life at the circus. One of the things that they tend to remember about seals is the way they can balance objects and the sounds they make. Although this activity places some tension on the arms, there is also a great deal of muscular rigidity of the legs. The emphasis is placed on keeping the legs as stiff as possible as the seal walks. This tension is released when the seal falls down.

> OLIVER OSTRICH
> There is a big bird at the zoo.
> His name is Oliver Ostrich.
> How could you look like Oliver Ostrich?
> I wonder if you could walk like Oliver Ostrich.
> Do you want to try?
> First, bend forward.
> Keep your knees straight.
> Hold your ankles.
> Now walk like Oliver Ostrich.
> Oliver Ostrich is tired.
> He sits down.

Description

In the **ostrich walk** the performer bends at the waist and grasps the ankles. Keeping the legs stiff and straight, he walks along in this position. If the performer cannot bend far enough to grasp the ankles, he bends as far as he can and grasps the legs at any point above the ankles.

Application

It is probably a good idea to begin the discussion by showing pictures of an ostrich. The main emphasis should be placed on the size of the bird and how it moves in comparison to other birds. In the **ostrich walk** much tension is placed on the muscles in the back and legs. This tension is released when the ostrich sits down.

With reference to the game and stunt stories, it is entirely possible that some teachers will want to try to develop some of their own stories, and it is heartily recommended that they try their hand at it. Should this be the case, the following guidelines are submitted for consideration.

1. In general, the **new** word load should be kept relatively low.
2. When new words are used, there should be as much repetition of these words as is possible and appropriate.
3. Sentence length and lack of complex sentences should be considered in keeping the level of difficulty of material within the ability level of children.

4. Consideration should also be given to the reading values and literary merits of a story. Using a character or characters in a story setting help to develop interest.
5. The activity to be used in the game and stunt story should **not** be readily identifiable. When children identify an activity early in the story, there can be resulting minimum attention on their part to get the necessary details to engage in the experience. Of course, the teacher plays a very important part in guiding the experience.

Chapter 7

RELAXATION THROUGH
CREATIVE MOVEMENT

IN ORDER TO provide the reader with an understanding of its meaning, it seems appropriate at the outset to provide a literal description of **creative movement**. The English word **creative** derives from the French word **createn** and the Latin word **creatus,** both of which mean "to bring into existence." The term **movement,** when applied to the human organism, simply means a "change in body position." Therefore, when we put the two words **creative** and **movement** together, the interpretation is bringing something into existence or being creative by expressing one's self by means of body movement.

One of the utmost concerns of educators in our modern democratic society is the problem of how to provide for creative expression so that a child may develop to the fullest extent of his potentialities. Democracy is only beginning to understand the power of the individual as perhaps the most dynamic force in the world today. It is in this frame of reference that creativity should come clearly into focus, because many of the problems in our complex society can be solved mainly through creative thinking.

Creative experience involves **self**-expression. It is concerned with the need to experiment, to express original ideas, and to think. Creativity and childhood enjoy a congruous relationship because children are naturally creative. They imagine. They pretend. They are uninhibited. They are not only original but actually ingenious in their thoughts and actions. Indeed, creativity is a characteristic inherent in the lives of practically all children. It may range from some children who create as a natural form of expression without teacher stimulation to others who may need varying degrees of teacher guidance and encouragement.

There are a variety of media for creative expression (art, music, and writing) that are considered the traditional approaches to creative expression; however, the very essence of creative expression is movement. Movement, as a form of creativity, uses the body as the instrument of expression. For the young child, the most natural form of creative expression is movement. Because of their very nature, children have a natural inclination for movement, and they use this medium as the basic form of creative expression. Movement is the child's universal language, a most important form of communication, and a most meaningful way of learning.

THEORY OF RELAXATION
THROUGH CREATIVE MOVEMENT

Relaxation through creative movement combines a form of imagery and tensing and releasing. (Imagery will be discussed in detail in the following chapter.) A child or group of children with various degrees of teacher guidance creates a movement(s) designed to tense and relax individual muscles, muscle groups, or the entire body. When this involves an individual muscle or a group of muscles, it can be called **specific** relaxation, and when it involves the entire body, it can be referred to as **general** relaxation. The procedure is applicable in the school setting to be used by the teacher. When used with one child or several children, the procedures are essentially the same.

Relaxation through creative movement simply means that there are contrasting creative movements that give the effect of tensing and letting go. Later sections of the chapter are devoted to providing a large number of creative movements for relaxation. Nevertheless, an illustration is provided here for a better understanding of the concept at this point.

This example shows the contrast (tensing and letting go) of the muscles in an upper extremity (arm). The teacher could start by raising a question, such as "What would you say is the main difference between a ball bat and a jump rope?" This question is then discussed with the children and will no doubt lead to the major difference being that a ball bat is hard and stiff and that a jump rope is soft and limp. The teacher might then proceed as follows:

> "Let's see if we can all make one of our arms be like a ball bat" (children create this movement). "Now quickly, can you make your arm be like a jump rope?" (children create the movement by releasing the tensed arm).

The experience can then be evaluated by using questions such as: "How did your arm feel when you made it like a bat?" and "How did your arm feel when you made it like a jump rope?"

The creative teacher along with the children can produce a discussion that will increase an understanding of the relaxation phenomenon. This is but one approach, and teachers are limited only by their own creativity and imagination.

SOME PRINCIPLES OF LEARNING APPLIED TO CREATIVE MOVEMENT

There are various basic facts about the nature of human beings of which we are now more cognizant than we were in the past. Essentially, these facts involve some of the fundamental aspects of the learning process, which all good teaching should take into account. Older concepts of teaching methods were based largely upon the idea that the teacher was the sole authority in terms of what was best for children, and that children were expected to learn regardless of the conditions surrounding the learning situation. For the most part, modern teaching replaces the older concepts with methods that are based on certain accepted beliefs of educational psychology. Outgrowths of these beliefs emerge in the form of principles of learning. The following principles provide important guidelines for arranging learning experiences for children, and they suggest how desirable learning can take place when the principles are satisfactorily applied to the teaching of creative movement.

1. **The child's own purposeful goals should guide his learning activities.** For a desirable learning situation to prevail, teachers should consider certain features about purposeful goals that guide learning activities. Of utmost importance is that the goal must seem worthwhile to the child. This will involve factors such as interest, attention, and motivation. Fortunately, in creative movement activities these factors are "built-in" qualities. Thus, the teacher does not necessarily need to "arouse" the child wih various kinds of motivating devices.

2. **The child should be given freedom to create his own responses in the situation he faces.** This principle indicates that **problem solving** is a very important way of human learning and that the child will learn mainly only through experience, either direct or indirect. This implies that the teacher should provide every opportunity for the child to use his

own judgment in the various situations that arise in the creative movement experience.

3. The child agrees to and acts upon the learnings that he considers of most value to him. Children accept as most valuable those things that are of greatest interest to them. This principle implies, in part, then, that there should be a satisfactory balance between **needs** and **interests** of children in their creative movement experiences. Although it is of extreme importance to consider the needs of children in developing experiences, the teacher should keep in mind that their interest is needed if the most desirable learning is to take place.

4. The child should be given the opportunity to share cooperatively in learning experiences with others under the guidance, but not the control, of the teacher. The point that should be emphasized here is that, although learning may be an individual matter, it can take place well in a group. This is to say that children learn individually, but that socialization can be retained. This can be achieved even if there are only two members participating, the teacher and the child.

5. The teacher should act as a guide who understands the child as a growing organism. This principle indicates that the teacher should consider learning as an evolving process and not just as instant behavior. If the teacher is to regard his or her efforts in terms of guidance and direction of behavior that results in learning, wisdom must be displayed as to when to "step in and teach" and when to step aside and watch for further opportunities to guide and direct behavior. The application of this principle precludes an approach that is teacher dominated. In this regard, the teacher could be guided by the old saying that "children should learn my monkeying and not be aping."

It is quite likely that teachers will have good success in using the creative movements in this chapter if they attempt to apply these principles. The main reason for this is that their efforts in helping children learn through creative movement will be in line with those conditions under which learning takes place most effectively.

CREATIVE MOVEMENTS FOR GENERAL RELAXATION

It was mentioned previously that general relaxation involves the entire body and that specific relaxation is concerned with an individual muscle or a group of muscles.

Specific relaxation as used here should not be confused with what some persons call **differential** relaxation. Those who use this term generally consider it to be concerned with relaxing all muscles except those that are actually needed for the particular occupation at hand. Perhaps it should be mentioned that the terms **general** and **specific** are used arbitrarily in the present discussions. This is to say that others may prefer to use different terms for this same purpose, and in the absence of standardized terminology, it is certainly their prerogative to do so. This section of the chapter is devoted to creative movements designed to relax the entire body (general), and the following section is concerned with creative movements for particular muscles or muscle groups (specific).

In considering the creative movement experiences that are recommended, it appears important to make some general suggestions for their use. The following descriptive list is submitted for this purpose:

1. Because of their very nature, most creative movement experiences tend to be relaxing. The reason for this is that they are conducted in an informal atmosphere with a minimum of formal structuring.
2. Although most children are naturally creative, some will manifest more creativity than others. This means that, depending upon the nature of a particular creative experience, along with the creative level of the child, there is a need to determine the extent of teacher guidance needed in each situation. With practice, most teachers will be able to make a judgment that is in the best interest of the children.
3. A very important aspect in conducting creative movement with children is the teacher's voice. The manner in which a teacher speaks, along with the intonation of certain words, can have a profound influence on children's creative responses. For example, a soft tone of voice tends to make children respond with a slower movement. A sharp or loud tone tends to cause children to respond more vigorously. Even the words can have an influence on children's responses. For instance, words like **hard** and **soft** and **heavy** and **light** are likely to inspire feelings and emotions that will result in varying responses. The important thing to keep uppermost in mind is that there should be a contrasting experience—tensing and letting go. The voice can have a pronounced influence on this experience.
4. The format for conducting the various activities is intended only as a general way of organizing the experiences. For this reason, the suggested procedures should be considered as a guide and not necessarily as a prescription to be followed. In other words, individuals

should inject their own creative ideas into the procedures for conducting the experiences. The suggested format consists of (a) the name of the activity, (b) suggested teacher input, (c) some possible children's responses, and (d) suggested evaluation procedures.

5. The question of **where** to conduct the activities is important. Most of them can be conducted while sitting at the desk. Others may require more space. The nature of the activity itself will ordinarily indicate where the activity might best take place.

Note: Creative movement responses of children are pretty much an individual matter; that is, each child is likely to respond in the way that the experience means to him personally. Therefore, a creative movement experience can be conducted with a group of children, with each child creating his or her own more or less unique response. At the same time, any of the recommended activities can be presented to a single child. Although the activities can be used with individual children or with groups of children, the indication in the description of the activities is that they are for a group of children.

Activity: Hard and Soft

A major purpose of this activity is to help the children distinguish between the terms **hard** and **soft.** The opening discussion can be oriented in this direction.

INTRODUCTION

The teacher can ask the children if they know the difference between hard and soft.

RESPONSES

Children might respond by naming some things that are hard or soft. (If this does happen, the teacher can guide the discussion with certain questions.)

TEACHER

"Is a rock hard?"
"Can you make a rock soft?"
"Is the pavement hard?"
"Can it be made soft?"
(The purpose here is to help those children who do not know the difference, or how to explain the difference, to be able to distinguish between hard and soft. All such questions will be governed by the original responses of the children.)

TEACHER

"We have talked about some of the things that are hard and some that are soft. Now, I wonder if you could do something to make yourself hard?"

RESPONSES

Children respond by creating shapes and positions that depict their bodies as being hard.

TEACHER

"Now, can you do something that will make your body feel soft?"

RESPONSES

Children do several things that give them the feeling of a soft body.

TEACHER

"All right. Very good. I am going to say the word **hard,** and when you hear it, I want you to make yourself feel hard. After that, I will say the word **soft** and then you make yourself feel soft."
(The teacher calls out the word **hard** and has the children hold their position for three or four seconds before calling out the word **soft.** This can be continued with the teacher using the words harder and hardest and softer and softest. The teacher should take advantage of appropriate intonation of the words **hard** and **soft**.)

EVALUATION

A discussion can be developed with questions such as the following:
"How did you feel when you were hard?"
"How did you feel when you were soft?"
"Did you feel better when you pretended you were hard or when you were soft?"
"Could you feel the difference?"

Activity: Cold and Hot

In working with children in creative movement, it has been found that there are certain conditions that cause children to react more or less "naturally" to specific situations. The activity **Cold and Hot** is a case in point. When children are asked to respond to **cold** they tend to react with a "tensed up" body condition. When responding to **hot** they tend to react with a more relaxed state. This is probably because children have had the actual experience of being cold and hot.

INTRODUCTION

The teacher can introduce the discussion by referring to certain climatic seasonal conditions that will depict cold and hot. Some introductory questions could include the following:

"Is a piece of ice hot or cold?"

"Is the sun hot or cold?"

"If you have been out on a cold winter day, how did it make you feel?"

"How does it feel to be outside on a warm summer day?"

"Can you think of some things that are cold or hot?"

(The teacher attempts to guide the discussion in the direction of a person's feelings when the body is cold and/or hot.)

RESPONSES

Some children are likely to suggest that they shiver when cold and sweat when hot. Others will tell about their experiences with things that are hot and cold.

TEACHER

"You have told a lot of things about cold and hot. Now, how would you like to show us how it feels to be cold and how it feels to be hot? When I say the word **cold,** please show us what you would do with your body. When I say the word **hot,** show us what your body would do."

(The teacher continues with this procedure as the children create body movements that express hot and cold.)

EVALUATION

"Did you feel 'looser' when you were cold or when you were hot? George, you made your body into a ball when I said 'Cold,' and when I said 'Hot,' you flopped over and spread out your arms. Why did you do that? Could you tell us the different feeling you had when you pretended to be cold than when you pretended to be hot?"

Activity: Giant and Dwarf

This activity focuses on what a child will do with his body when he tries to make himself larger and taller contrasted to when he tries to make himself smaller and shorter. It has been observed that, when children try to make themselves tall, more muscle tension occurs. On the contrary, when pretending to be short and small, there is a state of relaxation.

INTRODUCTION

The teacher can take many different approaches in introducing this activity. One would be to comment about the giants and dwarves in the circus. Many children have had the experience of either having been to a circus or having seen one on television.

RESPONSES

Children are likely to respond by commenting about the size of giants and dwarves and about how they move around — the giant with large steps and the dwarf with small choppy steps. They will also wish to imitate these movements.

TEACHER

"I wonder how it would feel to be big and tall like a giant? How do you think it would feel to be small and short like a dwarf? Maybe we should try it. I will say 'Giant,' then I will say 'Dwarf,' and you can pretend to be the one that I say. Are you ready?"
(The teacher alternates calling out "Giant" and 'Dwarf" as the children try to make their bodies into the particular designation.)

EVALUATION

"You did very well by changing quickly from a giant to a dwarf."
"Which was harder, being a giant or a dwarf?"
"How did your body feel when you tried to be a giant?"
"How did your body feel when you tried to be a dwarf?"
(In the evaluation the discussion might be guided in the direction that everyone should try to be comfortable being what he is and should be satisfied with himself regardless of whether he is large or small.)

Activity: Rain and Snow

This creative experience is like the previous ones; however, it differs because it is likely to be an experience in which most children have not participated on their own. It has been my experience that when children are asked to imitate rain, they tend to make their bodies tense. When imitating snow, they appear to relax the body. The reason for this could be that they generally associate rain as **heavy** and snow as **light.** Some teachers try to guide the discussion in this particular direction.

INTRODUCTION

One good way to introduce this activity is to ask what the difference is between rain and snow.

RESPONSES

Some typical responses are the following:
"Rain is wetter than snow."
"Rain comes down harder than snow."
"Snow is white; rain does not have color."
"It is more fun playing in the snow than it is in the rain."
"My mother doesn't care if I play in the snow, but she does not like to have me play in the rain."

TEACHER

"You have suggested some very interesting ways in which snow and rain are different. Now, how do you think it would make you feel to pretend you are rain — and then snow?"

RESPONSES

Children express different feelings.

TEACHER

"You have told many different ways it could feel to be like rain and snow. Now, let's pretend we are one and then the other. I will say 'Rain' and then I will say 'Snow.' "
(The teacher alternates calling out "Rain" and "Snow" as the children try to create movements in the form of these two elements.)

EVALUATION

"Which did you like best — pretending you were rain or pretending you were snow?"
"How did it feel to be like rain?"
"How did it feel to be like snow?"
"When did you feel more restful — when you were rain or when you were snow?"
"Did you feel heavier when you were rain?"
"Did you feel lighter when you were snow?"
"Which one gave you the better feeling?"

Activity: Peanut Butter and Milk

This activity is similar to the preceding one because the substances (peanut butter and milk) are concerned with contrasting consistency. Peanut butter is thought of as a thick substance, while milk is thought of as a thin substance.

INTRODUCTION

The discussion can be introduced by raising questions about the two foods as follows:
"How many of you drink milk everyday?"
"How many of you have eaten peanut butter?"
"What is the difference between the two?"
"What do you think would happen if we tried to pour peanut butter like we pour milk?"

RESPONSES

Children generally respond in terms of the thickness of peanut butter and the thinness of milk. Typical responses are the following:
"You don't spread milk like you do peanut butter."
"You can't make a sandwich out of milk."
"You eat peanut butter, but you drink milk."
"You can eat a peanut butter sandwich and then drink milk."

TEACHER

"Those are all good ideas. Now, how do you think it would feel to make your body like peanut butter and then like milk. Let's try it. I will say 'Peanut butter' and then I will say 'Milk,' and you try to change from one to the other."

EVALUATION

"How did you feel when you made yourself like peanut butter?"
"How did you feel when you made yourself like milk?"
"Was it easier to make yourself like peanut butter or like milk?"
"Which was more fun?"

Activity: Soldiers

In this activity the soldiers are depicted "at attention" and "at ease," or in a tensed and relaxed state. While children are likely to be familiar with the term **attention**, such is not likely to be the case with the term **at ease**. Therefore, in the discussion the teacher will need to focus on this, and the activity might be introduced as follows:

INTRODUCTION

"We talk a great deal about paying attention. What does this mean?"

RESPONSES

Some typical responses are:
"Listen when someone else is talking."
"Don't talk when you (teacher) are talking."
"Don't make noise."
"Do your work and don't fool around."

TEACHER

"You know pretty well what it means to 'pay attention.' Now, in something we are going to do we will use the word **attention.** How many of you have ever seen a soldier?"
(Some children indicate that they have, either in real life or on television or in the movies. The discussion focuses on what a soldier does when standing at attention and the children are asked to demonstrate.)
"Mary, can you show us how a soldier would look standing at attention."
(Several other children are asked to give their version of this and the teacher continues.)
"You all did very well. Now, soldiers do not stand at attention all of the time. Sometimes they are asked to stand 'at ease.' What do you think is meant by that?"
(Several children respond in various ways, and again, some are asked to demonstrate.)
"All right, let's try both of these, standing at attention and being at ease. I will first say one and then the other."

EVALUATION

The activity proceeds for a time and is followed by an evaluation using questions such as the following:
"How did it make you feel to stand at attention?"
"How did it make you feel to stand at ease?"
"Which was easier? Why?"

Activity: High Wire Walker

This activity is concerned with the tenseness experienced by the high wire walker when performing as compared to the relaxed state when dropping into a net.

INTRODUCTION

The activity can be introduced by simply asking how many children have seen a circus.

RESPONSES

Ordinarily, practically all children will have seen a circus, if not live, then on television.

TEACHER

"What are some of the things you like about a circus?"

RESPONSES

Obviously, there will be a large number and variety of responses. It will be very possible that one or more children will name the high wire performance. (If this is not the case, the teacher can guide the discussion to the high wire performance.)

TEACHER

"What are some things you would like to say about high wire walkers?"

RESPONSES

Some typical responses are as follows:
"They are almost at the top."
"They carry a long stick."
"They walk slowly."
"Sometimes they fall in a net."

TEACHER

(The teacher discusses the responses and continues).
"Let's try being high wire walkers and then we can pretend to drop into a net. When I say 'Walk,' you can pretend you are walking on the high wire. When I say 'Drop,' you can pretend to drop into the net."

EVALUATION

"What were some of the things you liked about being a high wire walker?"
"Did your body feel stiff when you were walking?"
"How did it feel when you dropped into the net?"
"Was it as much fun dropping into the net as it was walking on the high wire?"

Activity: The Kite

This activity is concerned with a kite in flight being kept up by the wind. This is compared to when the wind ceases and the kite begins to descend.

INTRODUCTION

In the introductory discussion, the teacher poses questions such as the following:

"What is a kite?"

"How many of you have ever had a kite?"

"Did you ever try to make a kite?"

"How can you make a kite fly?"

"What makes a kite stay in the air?"

"What happens when a kite begins to fall?"

RESPONSES

There will be many various responses, with the teacher attempting to guide the discussion in the direction of the purpose of the activity.

TEACHER

"How do you think it would feel to be like a kite up in the air?"

RESPONSES

Children express their feelings and the teacher encourages them to demonstrate. (Children will perform in many different ways, but the most prevalent way is taking a forward-leaning stance with arms outspread to the sides. This tends to cause the muscles of the body to become tense.)

TEACHER

"You are all very good at being a kite. Now, let's try being a kite in the air, kept up by the wind, and a kite after the wind stops blowing. When I say 'Up,' it will mean that you are a kite in the air, and when I say 'Down,' it will mean that the wind has stopped and the kite comes down."

EVALUATION

"How did you feel when you were a kite in the air?"

"How did you feel when the wind stopped?"

"What was the difference in your body when you were a kite in the air and when you were a kite when the wind stopped?"

Activity: The Balloon

This activity involves a balloon being blown up to capacity and then the air suddenly released. A very important feature of this activity is that it helps a child learn about controlled breathing, which is so important to muscular relaxation. This activity provides for rhythm in breathing as the child inhales deeply, then exhales, and becomes relaxed when the air is released from the balloon.

INTRODUCTION

To begin the discussion the teacher can use questions such as the following:

"Did you ever blow up a balloon and then let it go?"

"What happens if you blow it up too hard?"

"What happens when you let it go?"

(It may be a good idea for the teacher to start the discussion with a real balloon. It can be blown up and then let go, with the questions and discussion proceeding from this point.)

RESPONSES

Children will provide many responses verbally, but many times they will immediately try to show what a balloon does when it is let go with air in it.

TEACHER

"Good! You are acting like you are a balloon. Now, let's blow up like a balloon, and when I say 'let go,' everyone do what a balloon would do when the air comes out."

EVALUATION

"Did you feel tight when you took the air in like a balloon?"

"How did it make you feel when you were holding the air?"

"How did it make you feel when you let go?"

"Was it a better feeling to hold the air in or to let it go?"

Activity: Be This, Be That

This activity involves a series of contrasting creative movements. The teacher calls out a tension movement followed by a relaxation movement, with the children responding by creating the movements. The following are some possibilities for such movements, and the creative teacher along with the children will be able to think of many others:

Be a Telephone Pole — Be a Feather

Be an Icicle — Be a Pillow

Be a Statue — Be a Rubber Band

Be a Broom Handle — Be a Piece of String

Be a Chair — Be a Cushion

Be a Board — Be a Paper Bag

CREATIVE MOVEMENTS FOR
SPECIFIC RELAXATION

It might be useful to repeat the meaning of the terms **general** and **specific** relaxation. General relaxation is concerned with the entire body, while specific relaxation pertains to specific muscles or body parts. An interesting feature of specific relaxation is that it not only relaxes specific body parts but, at the same time, it makes it easier for the child to learn about the tensing-releasing phenomenon. It is easier to recognize this when just certain specific muscles are involved.

Most of the procedures recommended in the preceding section of the chapter apply here; however, the creative movements here will be organized under headings of specific muscle groups.

Muscles of the Head, Face, Tongue, and Neck

(Children particularly enjoy activities in this muscle group, because it gives them an opportunity to make "funny faces" legitimately).

Activity: Big Eye

In this activity the eyes are opened as wide as possible for a period of about four or five seconds. Also, the person can look to the right, left, above and below.

INTRODUCTION

The teacher can name the activity and ask the children what they think it means.

RESPONSES

Some children will immediately respond by opening their eyes very wide.

TEACHER

"When I say 'Big Eye,' try to open your eyes wide until I say 'Little Eye.' "

EVALUATION

"How did it feel to have a big eye? Did it feel different to have a little eye?"

Activity: The Sneeze

The muscles are contracted on either side of the nose as in sneezing. The skin should be wrinkled upward over the nose as hard as possible.

INTRODUCTION

The activity can be introduced by discussing how one looks when sneezing. There can also be a discussion of what causes one to sneeze.

RESPONSES

The children consider this to be a very funny activity and they will respond in a variety of ways. Some of them will immediately try to do a forced sneeze.

TEACHER

"I want you to show how you would look when you are getting ready to sneeze. When I say 'Ready,' everyone pretend to get ready to sneeze. When I say 'Sneeze,' everyone pretend to sneeze."

EVALUATION

"Did your face feel tight when you were getting ready to sneeze?"
"How did your face feel after you pretended to sneeze?"

Activity: Rabbit Nose

This activity involves dilating and flaring out the nostrils.

INTRODUCTION

The discussion can be introduced by considering how rabbits move, the color of their fur, and other features.

RESPONSES

Some children will have either had a pet rabbit or will have seen one in a pet store. They are very willing to tell many things that they know about them, because rabbits are a favorite of children.

TEACHER

(If none of the children respond about the quick movements that a rabbit makes with its nose, the teacher can point the discussion in this direction.)
"Have you ever noticed how rabbits make their nose move out and in? I wonder why they do this? Maybe we could pretend to be rabbits and make this movement with our noses. When I say 'Out,' pretend to make a rabbit nose. When I say 'Stop,' let your nose change back to the way it was before."

EVALUATION

"Did your nose feel tight when you made a rabbit nose? How did it feel when you let your nose change back?"

Activity: The Frown

There are many ways to perform this activity, which include: (1) stretching the left corner of the mouth up and out, (2) stretching the right corner of the mouth down and out, (3) stretching the left corner of the mouth down and out, and (4) stretching the lower lip down hard while trying to keep the lip flat.

INTRODUCTION

A discussion can begin about smiling and frowning, with consideration of how they are alike and different, why people smile and frown, and what it means to keep a "straight" face. Also, the teacher can mention the different kinds of frowns suggested above.

RESPONSES

While children will respond verbally, more often than not they will immediately respond by frowning or smiling.

TEACHER

"Let's play a game in which we will use different kinds of frowns. Remember the different kinds of frowns we talked about. When I say 'Frown,' make any kind of frown you please and hold it until I say 'Straight.' This means that you should quickly change from the frown to a straight face."

EVALUATION

"Was your face stiff when you frowned? Did your face feel loose when you changed from a frown to a straight face? What do you think happened?"

Activity: The Hard Whistle

The movement in this activity is with the lips, as in whistling, but it is done by tensing the lips vigorously.

INTRODUCTION

The discussion can begin by asking how many can whistle. This can be followed by a consideration of what causes the whistling sound.

RESPONSES

The responses can be noisy, because those children who can do so are likely to begin immediately to whistle.

TEACHER

"Did you notice the shape of your mouth and lips? They formed a circle. Now, let's try what we will call the hard whistle. What does that suggest to you?"

RESPONSES

Children give various comments on the position of the lips in the hard whistle.

TEACHER

"Let's try the hard whistle when I say 'Whistle.' When I say 'Stop,' let your lips go back to the regular position."

EVALUATION

"What kind of feeling did you have on your mouth and lips when you did the hard whistle? Did your lips feel tight? How did they feel when you stopped?"

Activity: The Silent Yell

In this activity the mouth is opened wide in any direction. This position is held until released.

INTRODUCTION

The teacher can start the discussion by mentioning that children call out to each other when they are playing outside. The question can be raised of what these calls are named.

RESPONSES

Children give these calls different names, and someone is likely to say they are yelling. If not, this can be mentioned by the teacher.

TEACHER

(The discussion can be continued by considering why people yell, as well as the sounds made by yelling. Finally, the discussion can be directed to the shape of the face when yelling).

"Now, let's try doing what we will call the silent yell. When I say 'Yell,' act like you are yelling, but do not make a sound. When I say 'Stop,' let your face return to the regular position."

EVALUATION

"Did your face feel stiff when you acted like you were yelling?"
"How did it feel when you stopped?"

Muscles of the Upper Extremities

Activity: The Squeezer

This activity involves squeezing an imaginary object. It is simply concerned with making a tightly clenched fist and then releasing to an open hand.

INTRODUCTION

The discussion can start with the teacher asking what is meant by the word squeeze, how the squeeze is accomplished, and under what conditions it is done.

RESPONSES

Children will give all sorts of responses, some of which include the following:

"You squeeze lemons."
"You squeeze tight on a bat when hitting a ball."
"I like to squeeze a toothpaste tube."
"I once squeezed a cherry and the seed popped out."

TEACHER

"There are certainly many things to squeeze and ways to squeeze them. The kind of squeeze I am thinking about is one in which you would use your whole hand to squeeze something, let's say like a rubber ball. Let's try it. When I say 'Squeeze,' everyone pretend to squeeze something in your hand. You can use both hands to pretend you have something in each hand. I will then say 'Open' and you can stop squeezing and let your hand come open."

EVALUATION

"Did your hands get tired when you squeezed hard? How did it feel when I said 'Open'?"

Activity: The Rubber Band

One way to be like a rubber band is to clasp the hand tightly in front of the chest with the elbow's pointing out to the sides. The idea of the rubber band is shown when the performer tries as hard as possible to pull the hands apart.

INTRODUCTION

A discussion can focus on rubber bands and their uses. Different-sized rubber bands can be presented and stretched to various lengths. (This is exciting for the children, because they wonder if the rubber band is going to break).

RESPONSES

Children will enter eagerly into a discussion about rubber bands, because practically all of them will have had some sort of experience with them.

TEACHER

"I wonder how it would feel to be a rubber band and stretch like one? Let's try some movements that would make us be like a rubber band."

RESPONSES

Children do a large variety of movements depicting a rubber band.

TEACHER

"I notice that some of you held your hands together like your arms were a rubber band."

(If this does not happen, it could possibly be suggested by the teacher.)

"Let's try to stretch the rubber band until it breaks. When I say, 'Start,' try to stretch very hard like a rubber band. When I say 'Snap,' pretend that the rubber band breaks."

EVALUATION

"Did your arms get tired quickly when you were stretching them like a rubber band? Did your hands and arms feel tight? How did it feel when I said 'Snap'?"

Activity: The Weight Lifter

This activity is concerned with lifting an imaginary weight while at the same time straining as if actually lifting a heavy weight. The kind of lift we are thinking of here is known as the "curl." The lifter stands upright. The weight is on the floor in front. The performer bends at the knees, stoops, and picks up the weight with both hands, "curling" it to the chest.

INTRODUCTION

The discussion can be introduced by asking what is meant by the term **weight lifter.**

RESPONSES

Since weight lifting has become a popular event, many children will have seen the activity on television. They are very interested in the strength it takes to lift the heavy weights.

TEACHER

(The discussion is focused on various ways to lift weights, with emphasis on the curl.)

"What do you think we mean when we say that one way of lifting a weight is the curl?"

RESPONSES

Some children will know immediately, and the discussion can be directed to why it is called the curl (weight is curled by the arms up to the chest).

TEACHER

"Let's see if we can be weight lifters and try the curl. When I say 'Curl,' pretend you are lifting a heavy weight. When I say 'Stop,' pretend to drop the weight."

EVALUATION

"Did your arms feel tight when you were lifting the weight? Did your arms get a tired feeling? How did it feel when the weight was dropped?"

Muscles of the Lower Extremities

Activity: Ankle Snap

In this activity the ankle is flexed (bent) very hard toward the body in order to stretch the muscles at the back of the legs from the knee down. This position is held for a short period and then the foot is extended outward for a short period. Finally, the position is released, relaxing the muscles. Each ankle can be flexed and extended separately.

INTRODUCTION

The discussion can center around the various extremities of the body with reference to how the different kinds of joints can bend (be flexed). The activity can be named and the teacher can ask what they think is meant by it.

RESPONSES

The kind of introduction mentioned above will likely result in many kinds of responses indicating experiences children have had with various body joints.

TEACHER

(The teacher takes into account the different responses and then attempts to direct these to the activity.)

"You have suggested many things that can be done with the ankles. Could you show us some of these things?"

RESPONSES

Children react with different ankle movements. If the teacher notices a movement similar to the ankle snap, this is pointed out.

TEACHER

"Let's play the ankle snap game. When I say 'Stretch in,' try to do this and when I say 'Stretch out,' try to do that. When I say 'Snap,' quickly stop stretching the ankle."

EVALUATION

"Did you stretch as hard as you could? How did it feel? Did you feel a change when I said 'Snap'? How did that feel?"

Activity: Kick Up

This activity is best accomplished from a sitting position in a chair or the edge of a desk. The sitting position should be such that the edge is under the knee. One leg is extended and held for a short period. The extended leg should be very stiff. After the short period, the leg is allowed to bend back to the original position. Each leg can be extended separately.

INTRODUCTION

The discussion can begin by asking about kicking as a movement. Particular reference can be made to its use as a skill in certain kinds of games.

RESPONSES

Children are likely to mention games in which the skill of kicking is used such as football, soccer, and the popular game of kickball played in many schools.

TEACHER

(After the discussion about kicking in general, the question is raised about kicking from a sitting position.)

RESPONSES

This will, of course, evoke many different reactions, because children will not be likely to think of kicking being used in this manner.

TEACHER

"There is an activity called **Kick Up.** What does this mean to you? Let's try it. When I say 'Kick up,' try doing this and hold it until I say 'Down.' "

EVALUATION

"How did it feel to kick up? Did your leg feel stiff? Did your leg get tired when you held it up? How did it feel when I said 'Down'?"

In summary, perhaps it should be mentioned that all of the activities presented have been field tested with many children. They have met with a great deal of success as a means of relieving tension.

The activities that have been suggested in this chapter should be considered as representative examples of an almost unlimited number of possibilities. These activities have numerous possible variations that will be immediately noticed by the discerning reader. Therefore, it is heartily recommended that these activities be used as a point of departure for the development of other creative movements for relaxation.

Chapters 4-7 have been concerned essentially with deep muscle relaxation and as such have had a physiological orientation. In the remainder of the book, other forms of relaxation are considered that are more psychological in nature.

Chapter 8

MENTAL PRACTICE AND IMAGERY

MENTAL PRACTICE is a symbolized rehearsal of a physical activity in the absence of any gross muscular movement. This means that a person imagines in his own mind the way he will perform a given activity. **Imagery** is concerned with the development of a mental image that may aid one in the performance of an activity. In mental practice, the person thinks through what he is going to do, and with imagery, he may suggest to himself (or another may suggest a condition to him) and he then tries to effect a mental image of the condition.

The use of mental practice in performing motor skills is not new. In fact, research in this general area has been going on for well over a half century. This research has revealed that imagining a movement will likely produce recordable electric action potentials emanating from the muscle groups that would be called up if the movement were to be actually carried out. In addition, most mental activity is accompanied by general rises in muscular tension.

One procedure in the use of mental practice for relaxation is that of making suggestions to one's self. For the most part, in early childhood, we first learn to act on the basis of verbal instructions from others. Later we learn to guide and direct our own behavior on the basis of our own language activities — we literally talk to ourselves, giving ourselves instructions. This point of view has long been supported by research that postulates that speech as a form of communication between children and adults later becomes a means of organizing the child's own behavior. That is, the function that was previously divided between two people — child and adult — becomes an internal function of human behavior.

An example is an approach recommended by C. Eugene Walker[1] involving one making relaxation-connected statements to himself or herself. He suggests the following specific illustration:

> I am going to relax completely. First, I will relax my forehead and scalp. I will let all the muscles of my forehead and scalp relax and become completely at rest. All of the wrinkles will come out of my forehead and that part of my body will relax completely. Now, I will relax the muscles of my face. I will just let them relax and go limp. There will be no tension in my jaw. Next, I will relax my neck muscles. Just let them become tranquil and allow all the pressure to leave them. My neck muscles are relaxing completely. Now, I will relax the muscles of my shoulders. That relaxation will spread down my arms to the elbows, down the forearm to the wrists, hands and fingers. My arms will just dangle from the frame of my body. I will now relax the muscles of my chest. I will let them relax. I will take a deep breath and relax, letting all the tightness and tenseness leave. My breathing will now be normal and relaxed, and I will relax the muscles of my stomach. Now, I will relax all the muscles up and down both sides of my spine; now, the waist, buttocks, and thighs down to my knees. Now, the relaxation will spread to the calves of my legs, ankles, and feet, and toes. I will just lie here and continue to let all the muscles go completely limp. I will become completely relaxed from the top of my head to the tips of my toes.

In discussing the use of imagery in relaxation with children, we need to make the differentiation between its use with systematic desensitization which will be taken into account in Chapter 10. With regard to the latter, it is a problem for some children to imagine the scenes in a hierarchy of anxiety-evoking stimuli. A reason for this is the preciseness of such scenes, because a child is given little latitude in "letting his mind wander." On the contrary, using imagery in relaxation is a joyful experience, while in systematic desensitization the child is asked to imagine scenes that provoke anxiety.

A number of research studies report success in using imagery as an aspect of relaxation with children. One study[2] used imagery to advantage on self-instructional training with hyperactive and impulsive children. In another study,[3] there was success with imagery in the development of a self-control program. A technique was developed to train disruptive children to have control by pairing imagery and relaxation.

---

[1] C. Eugene Walker, *Learn to Relax, 13 Ways to Reduce Tension* (Englewood Cliffs, NJ, Prentice-Hall, Inc., 1975), p. 5.

[2] F. Kanfer and A.P. Goldstein, *Helping People Change: A Textbook of Methods* (New York, The Pergammon Press), 1975.

[3] M. Schneider and A. Robin, *Turtle Manual* (Stony Brook, New York, Psychology Department, State University of New York, 1974).

In what he termed the "release only" phase of relaxation, Robert McBrien[4] used instructions involving imagery as follows:

> Just imagine you are lying on your back on soft green grass—you are so comfortable as you look up through the branches and leaves of a shade tree at the deep blue sky—you can see white soft puffy clouds floating by.
>
> (Further instructions to focus on the pleasant feeling of relaxation would then follow.)

Another way imagery can be used to promote a relaxed state is by making short comparative statements to children such as "float like a feather" or "melt like ice." In this regard, I would call your attention to the creative movement stories in the previous chapter. Stories of this nature can be used with imagery. The story is read and, with various degrees of teacher guidance, children try to depict the activity in the reading, selecting by creating their own responses and helping themselves to relax. The following is an example:

> SNOWFLAKES
> Snow!
> Snowflakes fall.
> They fall down.
> Down, down, down.
> Around and around.
> Could you move like snowflakes?

Two of my collaborators on a childhood stress project, the previously mentioned John Carter and Harold Russel, have prepared a tape called "Float Ride" which focuses on visual imagery. The following narrative is presented in a soft, slow and soothing voice, giving children plenty of time to listen, absorb and passively follow the directions. The dashes represent pauses. Soft music is in the background.

> FLOAT RIDE
> Now, get in a very comfortable position — — —
> Close your eyes and try to relax your body — — —
> Think about your breathing — — —
> Breathe in — — — Breathe out — — —
> Breathe in through your nose and out through your mouth — — —
> Now take a deep breath, hold it — — —
> Let it out slowly — — —

---

[4] Robert J. McBrien, Using relaxation methods with first grade boys, *Elementary School Guidance and Counseling* February (1978).

Feel yourself sinking deeper and deeper into the chair — — —

You're beginning to feel very comfortable and relaxed — — —

Today we're going to take a ride on a float in the Gulf. We each have a float and it needs to be blown up — — —

So first thing we do is blow them up. Take your float and blow into it, by taking deep breaths and exhaling into the float — — —

You will need to blow up your float at least ten times — — —

So now, take a very deep breath and, slowly exhale into your float — — —

Each time you breathe out, let your body become more and more relaxed — — —

Each breath should let you feel good inside — — —

Now that our floats are blown up, we'll walk down to the water — — —

The sun is very bright and it feels warm on your skin — — —

The sand feels warm and cushy and soft against your feet — — —

As we get closer to the water we can smell the salty air — — —

We can hear the waves — — — of the ocean as they hit the beach — — —

The water is closer now and the sand begins to get a little cooler — — —

The sun is shining on us and we feel good — — —

We will pause for a few moments now to feel the sun and the sand beneath our feet — — —

We are now at the edge of the water and we get on our floats — — —

The floats feel very comfortable and secure — — —

The air is warm and the water is cool — — —

We are slowly floating away from the shore on our floats and we feel very relaxed — — —

There are seagulls in the sky and we open our eyes to watch them fly by us — — —

The water is warm and we feel it with our hands and our legs — — —

The water is moving our floats away from the beach and we feel very comfortable and safe — — —

As the waves pass under us, the floats move slowly up, and slowly down — — —

We move with the floats — — — up, and down — — — up, and down — — — very slowly — — —

We feel as if we were being rocked to sleep — — —

The water is pushing us up and down — — — up, and down — — —

We feel very relaxed and comfortable — — —

As the waves are passing under us, they begin to pull us closer and closer and closer to the beach — — —

For just a few more seconds we can ride on our float without having to touch the sand — — —

The sun is warming our bodies, and the float ride is relaxing our bodies and our minds — — —

The floats touch the sand and we must get our bodies to move again — — —

So for a few seconds, bring yourself back to alertness and get off the float — — —

The sand feels warm against our feet once more and we feel very good inside and outside — — —

The air is warm and is drying our bodies quickly as we slowly walk away from the water — — —

Now we let the air out of our floats, and with each gust of wind escaping from the float we let it relax our bodies — — —

Now we have finished with the ride and with the floats and must return to the room — — —

As I count backward from five to one, slowly bring yourself back to being alert and relaxed — — —

5 — — —

4 — — —Begin to feel more alert and allow energy to come into your body — — —

3 — — —Move your arms and legs — — —

2 — — —Wiggle your fingers and your toes — — —open your eyes

1 — — —Sit up, stretch and feel alert and good all over.

A child stress management specialist who has had much success in using imagery to help children relax is Gretchen Koehler.[5] She has developed a number of routines for this purpose, some examples of which follow:

1. Take a walk in nature. Choose areas with soothing greens and cool blues. View distant objects, and also look closely at nature. Have your students lie on the grass and listen to natural sounds.

2. While sitting or lying down, imagine the warmth of the sun on your shoulders, arms, hands, legs, your whole body. Repeat phrases like, "Think about your hands; can you make them feel warm and heavy?" Teach the children to say to themselves, "I feel warm all over. I am calm and warm."

3. Count to ten aloud slowly while your students relax. Have them concentrate on slow breathing as they visualize the numbers. When the number ten is reached, the routine is over and students open their eyes and stretch.

---

[5] Gretchen Koehler, Stress management for children, *Strategies* Nov/Dec (1987).

4. Use of nature sounds has a relaxing effect on children. Play a tape of such sounds as birds, wind, streams, ocean waves, or rain. Instruct your students to listen and picture the place where they might hear these sounds.

5. Use quiet words to describe things that children can identify with and ask them to visualize as you speak. "Can you see a beautiful flower in your mind?" "Can you see a mountain or beach?"

6. Instruct your students to quietly repeat calm statements after you have said them. For instance: "I am calm;" "I am quiet;" "I feel relaxed."

In closing this chapter, a word of caution is submitted. Although mental practice and imagery are sound techniques for helping children relax, it is possible that with certain children there could be side effects. For example, a borderline psychotic child could possibly be harmed by imagery activities.

Chapter 9

THE QUIETING REFLEX

AN OUTSTANDING innovative approach to helping children deal with stress is the process known as the *Quieting Reflex* (QR). The technique was originated by Charles F. Stroebel, Director of Research, Institute of Living, Hartford, Connecticut. At the beginning, this approach was used exclusively with adults. Doctor Stroebel credits his wife Elizabeth and another associate, Doctor Margaret Holland, with modifying the technique for use with children.[1] (This version is known as Kiddie QR.)

Based on a solid foundation of objective evidence, Kiddie QR emphasizes the concept of the goodness of the body and "making friends with one's body." Essentially, it is considered an educational preventative health care program for helping children in the four- to nine-year age range deal with stress. The program is divided into 16 **experiential elements** on tapes of three to seven minutes in length. The tapes are accompanied by several booklets that explain in detail how to use the material. As an example, *Element Number* 16, "My very good feeling self," is designed to help a child understand that homeostasis is a state of physiological and psychological equilibrium. It reinforces the concept that the body is inherently good and that with care and the built-in safety mechanisms, each child can expect a healthy, happy life.

One of the very important dimensions of Kiddie QR is its emphasis on **mind/body integration** as a means of helping children understand about stress and what to do about it. Doctor Stroebel and his associates feel that children and adults alike confuse the common experience in daily life of being "psyched" and "hyped." They interpret the expression

---

[1] Elizabeth Stroebel, Charles F. Stroebel, and Margaret Holland, *Kiddie QR A Choice for Children* (Wethersfield, CT, 1980).

"psyched up" as a heightened mental state that may be likened to a positive enthusiastic state of healthy stress (eustress) or simple healthy excitement. The expression "hyped up" implies an excessive degree of body arousal, suggestive of nonproductive energy. Because of the pressures of daily living, it is easy to confuse these states and assume that both reactions are part of ongoing healthy behavior. For good health and development, it is essential to have access to the full spectrum of our emotional and physical reactions, to be aware of the subtleties in states or shifts in arousal level that are natural and that make us wonderfully unique.

In the Kiddie QR approach, a fairly simple illustration is used to help children grasp the complex idea of mind/body integration. This is the comparison between the interaction of emotional and physiological reaction in their bodies and the construction and operation of a toy car.

Car Frame	Bones
Radiator	Blood
Carburetor/Exhaust	Lungs
Pumps	Heart
Headlights	Eyes
Tires	Feet
Windows	Mouth/Breath
Brakes/Power	Muscles
Gasoline	Stress Hormones
Battery	Energy Source
Accelerator/Speedometer	Emotions

This comparison helps children conceptualize how the emotional arousal level mechanisms in the brain trigger off physiological reactions within the body.

In order for their toy race car to perform well, they must control the speed, check out the car and the track for problems, and keep an alert mind and calm body to keep the car functioning at optimal performance. A crucial factor is that of balancing moments of lower speed with moments of heightened acceleration through shifting into the appropriate speed gear. Similarly, children can learn that their body functions much like the mechanism and operation of a car and that their emotions act as the control center of their body frame, just as the accelerator pedal acts as the speed control of the car. And as in the car race, they recognize that the signaling mechanisms ready the body systems and organs to **gear up** to a higher arousal state when their emotional gas pedal or stress hormones alert their brain to do so, and when to **gear down** when their emotions signal the brain to slow down or lower the arousal.

It is felt that it is extremely important to emphasize the healthy aspect of these unique body mechanisms; that is, there are appropriate times to use our passing gear: for playing tag, racing on our bikes, and jumping up and down for joy when we are happy. Passing gear is a body safety feature for emergencies, too: when we are late for dinner and want to "step on the gas" so as to run quickly home, or for more serious problems when we need to move away from real danger. Within the discussion, the children can talk about why it would not usually be appropriate or safe to use our passing gear in the house where we might break something or hurt ourselves, or while we are trying to do our school work and the "wiggle" gear would interfere with mental performance.

One aspect of the approach, "QR and My Body Bike Cycle," is an experiential exercise in shifting body gears through learning to discriminate among the physiologic changes that can be observed and felt. For example, the children can observe changes in their breathing patterns, in feeling their heart rate accelerate, as well as by experimenting with overt muscle tensing. They experiment with arousal states by exploring appropriate and inappropriate "body speeds" by learning how to balance the emotions that accompany stressful situations with comfortable emotions and unstressful situations. In general, they learn that unnecessary wear and tear on the body diminishes performance and creativity. This exercise lends itself nicely to physically show how "hyper" or Type A tendencies are similar to keeping the body in passing gear all the time. The experiential work coupled with discussions is an avenue of communication that makes sense to children and is a way to talk about the consequence of these long-term patterns in a positive non-threatening framework so that the child need not become fearful or feel guilt.

The analogy of the car and the body helps a child visualize mind/body integration. Here is an appropriate place in discussing it with children to talk about how our emotions trigger off uncomfortable body sensations such as butterflies in the stomach, or a pounding heart, or the scary uneasy feelings that we experience without understanding their origins.

All of the *Elements* in the QR program are especially useful for children who display hyperactive behavior tendencies and who need a means to understand their body arousal state which is disquieting to them. By becoming aware of the mind/body integration concept, they can acquire practical skills and ways to discriminate their emotional and physiological speed and then how to adjust their mental and physical arousal levels for the task at hand.

RESEARCH IS SUPPORTIVE

As mentioned, Kiddie QR is based on a solid foundation of objective evidence. Controlled studies have demonstrated that QR is remarkably effective in classroom and clinical settings. The Mesa, Arizona school system was the first major school district to pioneer the QR program as early as 1979. The significance of this project under the direction of Doctor Richard Duncan, director of psychological services, lies in his early recognition that the effectiveness of any program must involve psychological services, prevention services, the superintendency, regular and special education teachers, as well as parents. Since this project began, over 850 school districts are addressing the stress needs of their staff and students.

A study was conducted by Disorbio[2] to examine the effectiveness of Kiddie QR on physiological, affective, and cognitive measures of anxiety in elementary school children.

Gender differences on all the variables were also assessed. Subjects in the study were 55 kindergarten through fifth grade elementary school children, 27 males and 28 females. An equal number of subjects served as a control group and did not receive the six-month relaxation training.

At pre- and post-training times, biofeedback instrumentation was utilized to measure forearm extensor electomyograph activity and right index-finger skin temperature, both before and after presentation of a stressor. The A-Trait Scale of the State-Trait Anxiety Inventory for Children determined levels of anxiety, and the Digit Span of the WISC-R measured ability to concentrate.

The pre- and post-training data were analyzed by two-way analyses of covariance. Significant and beneficial effects of the QR training were seen in children's ability to self-regulate relaxation before presentation of a stressor and in improved concentration. Gender differences appeared influential only for the prestressor assessment of forearm extensor muscle activity, as the boys obtained significantly lower readings, possibly indicating a movement artifact in this particular measure.

The findings of the study were seen as encouraging and indicative of the need for further exploration into the neglected area of relaxation methods and their effects on children's functioning.

---

[2] John Mark Disorbio, "The effects of the Kiddie Quieting Response on stress and anxiety of elementary school children" (Doctoral diss., University of Northern Colorado, Greeley, CO, 1983).

In another study by Danielson[3] involving the quieting reflex, 16 elementary school counselors received training on the theory and use of the quieting reflex and success imagery. Over a period of two years, fifth graders were instructed in the use of QR to reduce stress and anxiety. The children received success imagery training about an upcoming standardized science achievement test. Comparisons of test results with those of untrained controls indicated that trained subjects outperformed controls significantly in the first year and by a lesser degree in the second year.

As successful as Kiddie QR has been, the creators of the program themselves feel it is not a panacea for all stress needs. They suggest, however, that whatever program is used with children, two factors must be considered or the program will most likely fail over the long term. These factors are compliance and transfer of training. Compliance in Kiddie language means "sticking to what you are doing." Programs that impose time restrictions for best results or "drop out" activity have low compliance. Children drift away from the technique. Teaching techniques must be built into the program to ensure transfer of training. Core transference techniques means carry-over effect. Many potentially good programs fail to be implemented because they lack this vital component. The QR is a lifelong coping skill that goes with the adult and the child from the place of learning, whether at home or in school, to be used at the moment of stress anytime, anyplace. One does not need the therapist or teacher to be present to guide him or her through the motion. Once the response is learned, practice makes it automatic, a skill that stays with one forever. This is what is involved in transfer of training.

Teaching QR to children as a lifelong coping strategy may indeed change their "fate." Incorporating this health technique into their daily routine will most certainly affect the quality of their lives. How marvelous if prevention or health awareness were as significant a part of early childhood education as the three Rs. By teaching children positive, enjoyable ways to maintain wellness, an adult will give them a precious gift indeed — a chance to avoid or minimize the killer stress-related disorders of our generation. QR cannot eliminate stress in their lives, but it does teach children to appreciate happy, healthy stresses and to gain self-mastery over the effects of unhealthy stress on their bodies.[4]

---

[3] Harry A. Danielson, The quieting reflex and success imagery, *Elementary School Guidance and Counseling* December, 19 (1984): 152-155.

[4] Elizabeth L. Stroebel and Charles F. Stroebel, The quieting reflex: A psychophysiologic approach for helping children deal with healthy and unhealthy stress, in *Stress in Childhood*, ed. James H. Humphrey (New York, AMS Press, Inc., 1984), pp. 275-276.

Chapter 10

SYSTEMATIC DESENSITIZATION

SYSTEMATIC desensitization is a form of behavior modification and it can be described as the process of systematically lessening a specific learned fear in an individual. It is purported to provide one means of controlling anxiety. If one can accomplish this, it becomes an extremely important factor in reducing stress. The reason for this is that the individual becomes more able to control his fears and anxieties, rather than having them control him.

Credit for the development of the technique as a clinical procedure is ordinarily given to Doctor Joseph Wolpe,[1] a psychiatrist who is said to have introduced it for the purpose of reducing anxiety reactions.

From the point of view of a clinical psychotherapeutic procedure, systematic desensitization consists of presenting, to the imagination of the deeply relaxed person, the feeblest item in a list of anxiety-evoking stimuli repeatedly, until no more anxiety is evoked. The next item on the list is presented, and so on, until eventually, even the strongest of the anxiety-evoking stimuli fails to evoke any stir of anxiety in a person. It is the purpose of this chapter to provide information on this technique. At the same time, consideration will be given to self-administration for the teacher as well as how teachers can use the technique to help control fears in children.

Originally, the focus of systematic desensitization was primarily on counselor-client, therapist-patient, or teacher-student relationships, and it was perhaps one of the most widely used behavior therapy techniques. In recent years, systematic desensitization has gained tremendous favor as a self-administered technique. Although the value of it as a means of lessening stress-provoking situations has not been completely established

---

[1] Joseph Wolpe, *The Practice of Behavior Therapy,* 2nd ed. (New York, Pergamon Press, 1973).

by behavioral scientists, some of the research findings are indeed encouraging. For example, studies have shown that systematic self-desensitization can be very effective in overcoming severe public speaking anxiety, test anxiety, and a host of other stress-invoking stimuli.

It has been suggested by one authoritative source[2] that systematic self-desensitization efforts are not likely to be harmful, even if they fail. However, self-desensitization should be approached as an experimental procedure and it should be discontinued if the course of anxiety reduction is not relatively smooth, and it should be discontinued immediately if any increase of anxiety is experienced.

Various behavioral therapists and clinical psychologists have set forth procedures for adults for the practice of systematic desensitization. One impressive model that seems to have universal applicability is one suggested by one of my former collaborators, Doctor C. Eugene Walker,[3] Chief, Pediatric Psychology, The University of Oklahoma Medical School.

The subject of systematic desensitization is introduced with the notion that many fears and anxieties that people experience are due to what are termed **conditioned reactions.** These conditioned reactions are identified as stimuli that occur together in our experience and become associated with each other so that we respond to them in the same way, or in a highly similar way, when they occur again. This is to say that if we are made anxious in the presence of certain stimuli, these same stimuli will make us anxious later when they occur, even if the situation in reality no longer poses an actual threat. An example is a person who may have had a number of experiences as a child in which a person in authority, such as a school principal, policeman, or guard, frightened him and perhaps punished him in some way. Such a person's reactions as an adult to one in authority may produce considerably more anxiety in him than the situation really warrants. This is because of his previous conditioning of strong anxiety to an authority figure.

Many of our emotions seem to be based on such conditioned reactions. And, these reactions are somewhat similar to reflexes, but they are learned rather than inherited. Their automatic or "reflexive" character, however, explains why it is difficult to discuss things rationally with someone who is emotionally involved in a situation. He is responding

---

[2] David L. Watson and Roland G. Tharp, *Self-Directed Behavior: Self Modification for Personal Adjustment* (Belmont, CA, Wadsworth Publishing Company, Inc., 1972), p. 179.

[3] C. Eugene Walker, *Learn to Relax, 13 Ways to Reduce Tension* (Englewood Cliffs, NJ, Prentice-Hall, Inc., 1975), p. 7.

more with his conditioned reactions to the present stimuli than relating to the actual realities of a situation.

The recommendation for overcoming fears and anxieties in the form of conditioned reactions is the use of systematic desensitization, and a highly persuasive case can be made for its effectiveness, provided it is done properly.

DESENSITIZATION FOR TEACHERS

For most teachers the procedure for systematic self-desensitization is a relatively uncomplicated one. After a particular problem has been identified, the process consists of three sequential steps: (1) developing a hierarchy of anxiety-evoking stimuli, (2) complete relaxation, and (3) desensitization sessions. Using the previously mentioned authority figure as an example, let us make application of this to a teacher who has difficulty with this problem where relationship with the principal is concerned.

The first step is to take several index cards, writing a different situation or experience on each card that make for anxiety concerning the problem. The cards are then stacked in order, with the one causing the least anxiety on the top and the one causing the greatest anxiety at the bottom. This hierarchy of anxiety-evoking stimuli might resemble the following:

1. Entering school parking lot and seeing principal's car.
2. Greeting co-workers and discussing principal.
3. Greeting co-worker and co-worker mentions her coming meeting with the principal.
4. Conferring with co-workers on a meeting time with the principal and co-workers.
5. Walking by principal's office when door is closed.
6. Walking by principal's office when door is open (no verbalization or eye contact).
7. Walking by principal's office or meeting principal in hall and greeting principal.
8. Arranging meeting with principal.
9. Prearranged meeting with principal with many present, such as a committee meeting.
10. Prearranged meeting with principal with only self and principal present.

Another possible stress-inducing situation could be one in which a given student's behavior produces stress for the teacher. A hierarchy that the teacher might use for self-desensitization could be as follows:

1. Anticipating student's presence in school before school begins.
2. Knowledge that student is present in school and will be in class.
3. Anticipating behavior problem during day with the student.
4. Greeting student at the door in the morning.
5. Minor behavior problem arises and is resolved.
6. Minor behavior problem arises and is not resolved.
7. Major behavior problem arises and is resolved.
8. Major behavior problem arises and is not resolved.
9. Verbal or physical confrontation with student in front of class.

Of course, the reader must understand that the above hierarchies of anxiety-evoking stimuli are general in nature, and each individual would make out his or her own list in more specific detail.

The second step is to try to develop a condition of complete relaxation (the reader is referred back to Chapter 4 for deep muscle-relaxation procedures). It is recommended that the person go through each of the muscle groups in sequential order to learn to relax them one by one.

After the person is completely relaxed, the next step is the beginning of systematic self-desensitization. This is done as follows: Look at the top card on the pile — the one that is least anxiety provoking. Close the eyes and using the imagination, visualize as vividly as possible the situation described on it. That is, one imagines the situation occurring and that he or she is actually there. At this point, if some anxiety is experienced, the imaginary scene should cease immediately and the person should go back to relaxing. After complete relaxation is again obtained, the person is ready to proceed. This procedure is continued until the scene can be imagined without anxiety. This may take only one or two times, or it could take 15 to 20 times, but it should be repeated until no anxiety is felt. The entire procedure is continued until one has gone through all the cards.

It is recommended that one work on the scenes in this manner for approximately one half hour at a time. It can be done daily, every other day, or a couple of times a week, depending upon the amount of time one is willing or able to spend and how quickly one wants to conquer the anxiety. It appears to be a good practice to overlap one or two items from one session to another; that is, beginning a session by repeating an item or two from the previous session that were imagined without anxiety.

One variation of the above procedure is to tape record a description of each scene in advance. One then relaxes and listens to the tape. If anxiety appears, the recorder is turned off and the person goes back to relaxing. When relaxation is again accomplished, the individual proceeds as before. A value of using the tape recorder is that there is likely to be better pronunciation, enunciation, and intonation of words. In addition, it may be easier for the individual to concentrate, since he has provided his own auditory input on tape and does not have the additional task of verbalizing and trying to concentrate on the scene at the same time. If desired, the sequence of relaxation procedures can be taped as well.

After one has been desensitized, he can review in his own mind the preferred action to take in the situation that caused anxiety. Plans can then be made to do the right thing the next time the situation occurs.

Obviously, the success one experiences with this procedure will depend largely upon the extent to which one is willing to make the painstaking effort involved in the approach. Many persons who have tried it have been so delighted by its effects that they have deliberately sought out situations that previously had caused them great anxiety, frustration and failure. This is certainly a true test of faith in the approach.

DESENSITIZATION FOR CHILDREN

Systematic desensitization has been used with success in terms of lessening fears and anxieties among children. An example of such an experiment is one in which a six-and-one-half-year-old boy was unsuccessful in classroom verbalization.[4] Medical and psychiatric reports did not show any known reason for his unwillingness to talk in the classroom. Although the child's test results revealed that he had ability above average, his school progress failed to reach his level of potential. A six-week desensitization program of two sessions per week was developed to try to reduce or eliminate his fear of verbalization in class. The following hierarchy of anxiety-evoking stimuli was used in the experiment:

1. Reading alone to investigator.
2. Reading alone to roommate.
3. Reading to two classroom aides.
4. Reading to teacher and classroom aides.

---

[4] R. Kravetz and S. Forness, The special classroom as a desensitization setting, *Exceptional Children* 37:389-391.

5. Reading to teacher, classroom aides, and small groups of class peers.
6. Reading to entire class.
7. Asking questions or making comments at weekly meetings when all children, teachers, and staff were present.

This program of desensitization met with success in alleviating the child's fear of verbalization in the classroom. Other programs of this same general nature have been used to advantage in reducing test-taking anxiety, conquering the phobia of school attendance, fear of medical settings, fear of darkness, water, and insects; in fact, most fears of children can be alleviated by systematic desensitization if the procedure is carried out properly.

With reference to conquering the phobia of school attendance, it has been found that many school children who are not reading and writing as well as they should may be just too frightened to do any better.[5]

Many of the phobias connected with reading and writing result from conditioned reactions. After a time, the original problem may be resolved, but the barrier to learning which was removed has been replaced by another one, the phobia. Since the child could not read or write well, he was probably a failure in school. Children may associate reading and writing with failure, and most of them are afraid of failing. In time, the fear can grow and the child really needs help. It has been demonstrated that this help almost always comes by systematically desensitizing the fear.

Although systematic desensitization has proved to be a very successful procedure to use to desensitize children to fear, its use as a "self"-administering device is not always applicable for fairly obvious reasons. This means that the child does not make up his or her own hierarchy of anxiety-evoking stimuli, but on the other hand, this is done by the teacher, sometimes in collaboration with the child.

Although some fears are serious enough to warrant clinical intervention by a professional therapist, in many instances a teacher can be successful in the use of systematic desensitization with children. As a matter of fact, parents, without even being aware of it, sometimes actually practice systematic desensitization with their children. Take, for example, the first trip to the beach: a child may have a fear not only of the water but of the noise and vastness of the environment as well. A parent may desensitize the child's fear by unknowingly practicing the

---

[5] C. Eugene Walker, Phobias hamper school children, *Oklahoma Journal* June 6, 1977.

following hierarchy of anxiety-evoking stimuli. The child, accompanied by the parent, may play near the water for a time. Next, one foot is placed in the water, followed by both feet immersed to the ankles, then to the thighs, waist and finally immersion up to the neck.

Another example where a parent may unwittingly practice systematic desensitization with a child is when there is a fear of the dark. The child may be permitted to sleep with a light on in his room for several nights. This is followed by turning out the light in the child's room but leaving one on in a nearby room with the door left open. On successive nights, the door is closed more and more until the fear is eliminated and the child is encouraged to sleep with the light off and the door closed.

If systematic desensitization is to meet with success when applied to children, there are certain considerations that need to be taken into account. Most of these concerns center around the level of cognitive development of the child. In this regard, I have already mentioned the responsibility the teacher should take in developing the hierarchy of anxiety-evoking stimuli.

Another cognitive factor to consider is the extent to which a child can apply his or her imagination to the stress-invoking scenes implied in the hierarchy of anxiety-evoking stimuli. In this particular regard, the late Jean Piaget,[6] the world famous child development specialist, felt that developmentally imagery is thought to first occur in late infancy when "deferred imitation" takes place. Mental imagery apparently cannot occur before this time. In "deferred imitation" the child is able to distinguish a mental image from the actual event it represents. However, Piaget felt that the image is very specific to the event it is imitating and is concrete rather than conceptual. Therefore, it is questionable whether four- or five-year-old children can manipulate imagery in the ways required for systematic desensitization. It has also been suggested that the younger child may be able to attend to only a limited number of characteristics of the stimulus because of his or her stage of development.[7]

It could be that using such a procedure in place of imagining scenes may be best for these children. For example, in what is called *in vivo* desensitization, the child can use toys to play out a hierarchy of fear situations, or the child can be allowed to draw the feared scenes.

---

[6] Jean Piaget, *Les Mecanismes Perdeptifs* (Paris, Presses, Universitares de France, 1961).

[7] J. Bruner, Image and symbol in development of magnitude and order, in *The Causes of Behavior: Readings in Child Development and Educational Psychology,* ed. J.F. Rosenblits and W. Allinsmith, (Boston, Allyn & Bacon, Inc., 1969).

In this general connection, the following series of steps involving a child's fear of birds is recommended by Barbara Kuczen.[8]

Step 1. Determine exactly what is fearful to the child. Encourage the child to talk about and explore the cause and nature of the problem. Do not (1) take the fear lightly, (2) ridicule, (3) attempt coercion (e.g. "Don't be afraid, touch the birdie"), or (4) ignore the problem. Logical explanation can help, but do not expect to explain away the fear.

Step 2. If possible, arrange for the child to see others happy and safe in the situation he or she fears.

Step 3. Arrange for carefully supervised contact with the fear, during which you provide positive support and understanding. This procedure involves desensitization and might work as follows:

a. Look at pictures of birds. Discuss whether or not a bird could actually harm you.

b. Have the child hold a toy bird of some type, a plastic model, for example, or a stuffed animal.

c. Let the child watch a friend caring for and holding a pet parakeet. (Take care that the bird is a gentle one.)

d. Have the child watch the parakeet in its cage.

e. Tell the child to touch the parakeet briefly as the friend holds it.

f. Have the child hold the parakeet for five seconds with a pair of gloves on.

g. Have the child hold the parakeet for ten seconds with a pair of gloves on.

h. Have the child hold the parakeet for five seconds with bare hands.

i. Have the child hold the parakeet for ten seconds with bare hands.

j. Have the child hold the parakeet in lap and pet it.

What is called "anticipatory imagery" develops around age seven or eight. The imagery allows for manipulation of the mental representation so that it can be moved about in space or changed in form. It is plausible that seven- and eight-year-olds could use systematic desensitization effectively. However, not too many studies using traditional systematic desensitization have been done with children under ten years of age. With many children, reinforcement may also be necessary to motivate the child to attempt and then practice visualizing.[9]

---

[8] Barbara Kuczen, *Childhood Stress, Don't Let Your Child be a Victim* (New York, Delacorte Press, 1982), p. 149.

[9] D'Ann Whitehead, Mariela Shirley, and C. Eugene Walker, Use of systematic desensitization in the treatment of children's fears, in *Stress in Childhood*, ed. James H. Humphrey (New York, AMS Press, Inc., 1984), p. 220.

It is important to recognize that some authorities contend that the concrete images used by children below age seven or eight have a high degree of affect associated with them. This means that there should be caution in the use of imagery of an aversive nature, due to the possibility that the child might imagine such an aversive scene and experience further trauma rather than alleviation of the fear.[10]

Another factor to take into account when using systematic desensitization with children is the extent to which they are able to learn to relax in a short period of time. Of course, if relaxation procedures are presented to children in the same manner as they are for adults, they might have difficulty in learning how to relax. In my own work I have never encountered this problem, because the techniques recommended in this book have always met with success.

In those cases where teachers do have difficulty getting children to relax, a technique called "emotive imagery" has been used with success for many years. This technique replaces relaxation as the anxiety-inhibiting response in systematic desensitization. It is meant to arouse feelings of bravery, pride, and assertiveness in the child. Like systematic desensitization, a graduated hierarchy of child's fears is developed. However, instead of imagining the scene concurrent with relaxing, the child is guided by the teacher in the imagery of the feared scene with credible events woven around a favorite hero. This could be one of the Muppets, a cartoon character or a television hero.[11]

In summary, it should be emphasized that when a given procedure can be used satisfactorily with teachers, it does not follow automatically that it will be successful with children if used in the same way. Therefore, teachers should exercise judgment and caution when making application of systematic desensitization with children.

---

[10] C.H. Elliott and M. Ozolins, Use of imagery in treatment of children, in *Handbook of Child Clinical Psychology,* ed. C.E. Walker and M. Roberts (New York, John Wiley & Sons, 1983).

[11] A.A. Lazarus and A. Abramovitz, The use of emotive therapy in the treatment of children's phobias (*Journal of Mental Science,* 108:191-195).

Chapter 11

MEDITATION

THE EASTERN art of meditation dates back more than 2,000 years. Until recently, this ancient art has been encumbered with religious as well as cultural connotations. In the 1960s, countercultures began using it as a route to a more natural means of living and relaxing. Today, persons from all walks of life can be counted among the untold numbers around the world who practice and realize the positive effects that meditation can have upon the human mind and body. This chapter will take into account various aspects of meditation, including information about a procedure that can be easily learned and practiced for the purpose of reducing stress and tension. Consideration will be given to how teachers can practice meditation and how it can be used effectively to reduce tension in children.

It has been asserted by Kenneth Pelletier[1] that meditation should be defined as an experimental exercise involving an individual's actual attention, not belief systems or other cognitive processes, and that it should not be confused with prolonged, self-induced lethargy. The nervous system needs intensity and variety of external stimulation to maintain proper functioning.

The present chapter involves "mind" relaxation. The theory involved in meditation is that if the mind is quieted, then other systems of the body will tend to become stabilized.

Although there are many meditation techniques, **concentration** is a very essential factor contributing to success. The mind's natural flow from one idea to another is quieted by the individual's concentration.

---

[1] Kenneth R. Pelletier, *Mind As Healer Mind As Slayer* (New York, Dell Publishing Co., Inc., 1977), p. 192.

Lowering mental activity may be an easy task, but almost total elimination of scattered thoughts takes a great deal of time and practice on the part of the meditator.

The question sometimes raised is, Are Sleep and meditation the same thing? Sleep has been likened to meditation, as both are hypometabolic states — that is, restful states where the body experiences decreased metabolism. But meditation is not a form of sleep. Although some similar psychological changes have been found in sleep and meditation, they are not the same and one is not a substitute for the other. In this regard, it is interesting to note that various studies have shown that meditation may restore more energy than sleep.

There have been countless positive pronouncements about meditation from some of the most notable scientists of modern times who spend a good portion of their time studying about stress. However, it has been in relatively recent years only that the scientific community has uncovered many of the positive effects that the repeated practice of meditation has upon those who are stress ridden. Various scientific studies have shown that meditation can actually decrease the possibilities of an individual contracting stress-related disorders, and that meditators have a much faster recovery rate when exposed to a stressful situation than non-meditators. Specifically, from a physiological point of view, Herbert Benson[2] has found that meditation decreases the body's metabolic rate, with the following decreases in bodily function involved: (1) oxygen consumption, (2) breathing rate, (3) heart rate and blood pressure, (4) sympathetic nervous system activity, and (5) blood lactate (a chemical produced in the body during stressful encounters). Also, meditation tends to increase the psychological stability of those who practice it, as well as to reduce anxiety.

TYPES OF MEDITATION

Although there are many meditation techniques, one notable stress researcher, Daniel Goleman,[3] has stated that research tends to show that one technique is about as good as another for improving the way we handle stress.

---

[2] Herbert Benson, *The Relaxation Response* (New York, William Morrow and Company, 1975), p. 68.

[3] Daniel J. Goleman, Meditation helps break the stress spiral, *Psychology Today* February (1976).

Of the various types of meditation, transcendental meditation (TM) is by far the best known. It was introduced into the United States by Mararishi Mahesh Yogi. It is believed that he used the term **transcendental** (a literal meaning of which is "going beyond") to indicate that it projects one beyond the level of a wakeful experience to a state of profound rest along with heightened alertness.[+]

TM involves the repetition of a **mantra** (a word or specific sound) for 15 to 20 minutes daily with the meditator in a relaxed position with closed eyes. Almost without exception those who have practiced TM attest to its positive effects. While other forms of meditation may have specific procedures, it is safe to say that most derive in some way from basic TM.

A PROCEDURE FOR MEDITATING
FOR TEACHERS

Presented here is a description of a procedure for meditating that has met with personal success. However, it should be mentioned that it is pretty much an individual matter, and what may be successful for one person may not necessarily be successful for another.

To begin with, there are certain basic considerations that should be taken into account. The following descriptive list of these considerations is general in nature, and the reader can make his or her own specific application as best fits individual needs and interests.

Locate a quiet place and assume a comfortable position. The importance of a quiet environment should be obvious, since concentration is facilitated in a tranquil surrounding. The question of the position one may assume for meditation is an individual matter. However, when it is suggested that one assume a comfortable position, this might be amended by "but not too comfortable." The reason for this is that if one is too comfortable, there is the possibility of falling asleep, and this of course would defeat the purpose of meditation. This is a reason why one should consider not taking a lying position while meditating.

A position might be taken where there is some latitude for "swaying." This can provide for a comfortable posture and, at the same time, guard against the individual's "falling into dreamland." The main consideration is that the person be in a comfortable enough position to remain this way

---

[+] Harold H. Bloomfield et al., *TM Discovering Inner Energy and Overcoming Stress* (Boston, G.K. Hall & Co., 1976), p. 7.

for a period of 15 minutes or so. One such position would be where you sit on the floor with legs crossed and back straight and resting on the legs and buttocks. The head should be erect and the hands resting in the lap. If you prefer to sit in a chair rather than on the floor, select a chair with a straight back. You need to be the judge of comfort, and, thus, you select a position where you feel you are able to concentrate and remain in this position for a period of time.

Focus your concentration. As mentioned before, concentration is the essential key to successful meditation. If you focus on one specific thing, such as an object or sound or a personal feeling, it is less likely that your thoughts will be distracted. You might want to consider focusing on such things as a fantasy trip, re-experiencing a trip already taken, a place that has not been visited, or a certain sound or chant.

Use of a nonsense word or phrase. Some techniques of meditation, such as the popular TM, involve the chanting of a particular word (mantra) as one meditates. While the mantra has important meaning for the meditator, it is referred to as a nonsense word because it should be devoid of any connotation that would send one thinking in many directions. This, of course, would hinder concentration, so a nonsense word would perhaps be most effective.

Be aware of natural breathing rhythm. The importance of natural breathing rhythm should not be underestimated. In fact, some clinical psychologists recommend this as a means of concentrating. That is, one can count the number of times he or she inhales and exhales, and this in itself is a relaxing mental activity.

The time for meditation. Since meditation is an activity to quiet the mind, it is strongly recommended that the practice not be undertaken immediately upon arrival home from work. At this time, the mind may be in a very active state of reviewing the day's activities. Personal experience suggests a 15- to 20-minute period in the morning before work and another such period in the evening, preferably before dinner or possibly two hours after dinner.

With the above basic considerations in mind, you should be ready to experiment. To begin with, assume a comfortable position in a quiet place with as passive an attitude as possible. Try to dismiss all wandering thoughts from your mind and concentrate on a relaxed body while keeping the eyes closed. When feeling fairly relaxed, the repetition of the nonsense word or phrase can begin. This can be repeated orally or silently; that is, through the mind. Repeat your chosen word or phrase in this manner over and over, keeping the mind clear of any passing thoughts. At first, this may be difficult, but with practice it becomes easier.

After a period of about 15 to 20 minutes have passed, discontinue repetition of the word or phrase. Become aware of your relaxed body once again. Give yourself a few moments before moving, as your body will need to readjust. For successful prolonged results one might consider continuing the practice two times daily for 15- to 20- minute sessions.

If you have difficulty trying to meditate on your own, it is possible to seek the services of an experienced meditator for assistance and supervision. The recent widespread popularity of meditation has been accompanied by the establishment of meditation centers for instruction in some communities.

MEDITATION FOR CHILDREN

There is a great deal of available evidence to support the idea that the practice of meditation is very beneficial to children. All family members can learn meditation techniques, and children as young as ten years of age can learn, though they meditate for less than 15 minutes. Often, younger children become interested in learning to meditate after others in the family have begun practicing the technique.

In Hartford, Connecticut, courses in the technique of transcendental meditation have been prepared for primary level children and implemented by some teachers. Among other things, it is reported that this program improves creativity, and that perhaps child psychologists should investigate the effect of the children's technique of TM on early development and creativity. With regard to the latter, Gowan[5] studied the facilitation of creativity through meditation. He reviewed the emerging concepts of creativity along with therapeutic procedures designed to relieve the mental blocks caused by anxiety and stress. Various research studies on the use of TM to increase creativity, decrease anxiety and control stress have suggested that children could be helped to obtain greater creativity through knowledge of one or more meditation techniques.

Work by Rozman,[6] based on actual experience in teaching the science of meditation to children 3-13 years of age, has been shown to

---

[5] John Curtis Gowan, The facilitation of creativity through meditation procedures, *Journal of Creative Behavior* 12:156-160.

[6] Deborah Rozman, *Meditating with Children: A Workbook on New Age Educational Methods Using Meditation* (Boulder Creek, CA, University of the Trees Press, 1976).

help make group work with children peaceful, integrated and meaningful. In addition, children are assisted to resolve personal problems and stresses. Moreover, she found that meditation can be used successfully with gifted, retarded, average or hyperactive children.

Some very interesting research has been done with regard to attentiveness of children. Murdock[7] describes an approach used by an elementary school teacher to teach meditation exercises to a class of 25 normal and highly gifted kindergarten children. Breathing exercises and the tensing and loosening of muscles were used before going into the process of meditation. Feedback from children themselves seemed to suggest increased levels of attention span.

In another study involving attention, Redfering[8] had 18 children, 8-11 years old, participate in either the treatment group and practice Herbert Benson's meditative-relaxation technique or in the non-treatment group, relaxing for the same 20-minute sessions over a five-day period. Non-attending behavioral levels were recorded during the treatment period. Mean change differences of non-attending behaviors for the two groups reflected a significant reduction in the number of non-attending behaviors for the treatment group.

A study concerned with attention deficit disorder with hyperactivity was conducted by Kratter and Hogan.[9] A total of 24 children, meeting several criteria for being diagnosed as having an attention deficit disorder with hyperactivity, were selected for the study. Children were assigned to one of three conditions: a meditation-training group, a progressive-muscle relaxation group, or a waiting list control group. Subjects in the training groups were seen on an individual basis for 20 minutes twice weekly for a period of four weeks. Meditating subjects sat with eyes closed, breathed slowly, and deeply, and repeated the Sanskrit word "ahnam" ("nameless") first aloud and then silently for periods gradually increasing in duration from two to eight minutes. Relaxing subjects tensed and relaxed hands, forearms, biceps, triceps, shoulders, stomach, thighs, and calves in periods increasing from two to eight minutes. Results indicated that both the meditation-training and relaxation-training groups showed significant decreases in levels of impulsivity. No change in impulsivity was found in the control group. In the measures of selective

---

[7] Maureen H. Murdock, Meditation with young children, *Journal of Transpersonal Psychology* 10:29-44.

[8] David L. Redfering, Effects of meditative-relaxation exercises on non-attending behavior of behaviorally disturbed children, *Journal of Clinical Psychology* 10:126-127.

[9] Jonathan Kratter and John D. Hogan, The use of meditation in the treatment of attention deficit disorder with hyperactivity, *RIE* December (1983).

deployment of attention and freedom from distractibility, only meditation training resulted in a significant improvement in the behavior of
children in both the meditation-training and relaxation-training groups.
Parent rating scales reflected a significant improvement in the behavior
of children in both the meditation-training and relaxation-training
groups.

In the field of special education, Ferguson[10] reviewed research on the
physiological, perceptual and psychological benefits of the practice of
TM for potential applicability to exceptional children. Meditation was
seen to be of importance to education, in that it is reported to improve
learning, memory, grades, interpersonal relationships and cognitive perceptual functioning. It is suggested that meditation would be applicable
to exceptional or developmentally disabled children.

In an extensive study of mentally retarded Korean children Dong-
Keuk Kim[11] used Yoga exercises and dieting over a five-year period with
240 children with mental defects. The regimen also included meditation, physical training and breathing exercises. The program helped to
restore emotional stability and control behavior in addition to enhancing
physical posture. The number of problems decreased by 60 percent. A
general increase in scholastic performance was noticed. Participating
teachers and parents also profited from Yoga exercise and dieting.

This study is mentioned because meditation has long been an important concomitant ally with Yoga exercises. Rachel Carr[12] one of the foremost authorities on Yoga exercises for children, considers meditation a
very important "mental exercise" and feels that it can make a child a
more understanding and considerate person. She suggests that a child sit
in a quiet place where he or she will not be disturbed and begin to relax
the mind by breathing quietly with eyes closed. She asks children to concentrate on the rhythm of breathing so as to feel the breath rise and fall
while inhaling and exhaling through the nostrils. While listening to the
breath, the mind is turned inward and children are asked to meditate on
the following five principles:

1. Silence: When you are silent, you will still your mind.
2. Listening: When you listen, you learn.

---

[10] Phillip C. Ferguson, Transcendental meditation and its potential application in the field of special education, *Journal of Special Education* Summer (1976).

[11] Dong-Keuk Kim, The mentally retarded and Yoga, *Report of the Second Asian Conference on Mental Retardation* (Tokyo, Japan, League of the Mentally Retarded, 1975).

[12] Rachel Carr, *Wheel, Camel, Fish and Plow Yoga for You* (Englewood Cliffs, NJ, Prentice-Hall, Inc., 1981), pp. 29-30.

3. Remembering: When you remember, you become more considerate of others.
4. Understanding: When you understand, your actions will have more meaning.
5. Acting: Finally, when you act, it should be with a gentle heart and an understanding mind. Only then can you truly say that you are able to forgive those who have harmed you and that you are a better person for it.

The studies reported here comprise but a few of the large number that have been undertaken in the area of effectiveness of meditation for children. In most cases, these examples have shown a very positive effect of meditation. However, certain precautions need to be taken into account in interpreting the results, and the reader is reminded of possible limitations.

In closing this chapter, I would like to mention a television program that was observed recently. The program was called: "Special Treat: He Makes Me Feel Like Dancin'." At the end of the program some of the children were asked to give their reaction to it. One boy, perhaps nine or ten years of age, said, "It's a bit like meditation; you let your spirit run free."

And a final comment. More often than not children are reprimanded in school for "daydreaming." This is unfortunate because when one considers a daydream to be "a pleasant reverie of wish fulfillment," it could be a form of meditation whereby the child extricates himself from the cares and worries associated with the school day.

Chapter 12

BIOFEEDBACK

IN THIS discussion of biofeedback, it should be made luminously clear that we are dealing with a complex and complicated subject. It will be the purpose to discuss this phenomenon in terms of what it is supposed to be and what it is supposed to do. It should be borne in mind that (at least in the early stages of biofeedback training) (BFT) an important factor is that it take place under qualified supervision. This means that, should you wish to pursue an interest in and eventually participate in BFT, you should seek the services of one trained in this area.

THE MEANING OF BIOFEEDBACK

The term **feedback** has been used in various frames of reference. It may have been used originally in engineering in connection with control systems that involve feedback procedures. These feedback control systems make adjustments to environmental changes, such as the case of your thermostat controlling temperature levels in your home.

Learning theorists use the term feedback interchangeably with the expression **knowledge of results** to describe the process of providing the learner with information as to how accurate his reactions were. Or, in other words, feedback is knowledge of various kinds that the performer received about his performance. With particular reference to motor skill learning, some psychologists reported many years ago that feedback in the form of knowledge of results is the strongest, most important variable controlling performance and learning, and further, that studies have repeatedly shown that there is no improvement without it, progressive improvement with it, and deterioration after its withdrawal.[1]

---

[1] Edward A. Bilodeau and Ina Bilodeau, Motor skill learning, *Annual Review of Psychology* Palo Alto, CA, 1961.

According to Doctor Barbara Brown,[2] one of the foremost authorities on the subject of biofeedback, the terms **feedback** and **feedback control systems** were borrowed by physiologists when they began theorizing about how the functions of the body were performed. Modern writers on the subject of biofeedback seem to describe it essentially the same way, although some may elaborate more in determining its precise meaning. That is, some merely state what it is, while others may extend the description to include what it does. For example, one source[3] describes it as any information that we receive about the functioning of our internal organs such as the heart, sweat glands, muscles, and brain. Another similar description[4] indicates that it is a process in which information about an organism's biologic activity is supplied for perception by the same organism. Another source[5] extends this some by indicating that biofeedback is the monitoring of signals from the body, such as muscle tension and hand warmth, and the feeding of that information back through the use of sophisticated machines to individuals so they can get external information as to exactly what is happening in their bodies.

It has been estimated by the aforementioned Barbara Brown that there are perhaps millions of individual feedback systems in the human body. She comments that information about the external environment is sensed by any of the five senses and relayed to a control center, usually the brain, where it is integrated with other relevant information, and when the sensed information is significant enough, central control generates commands for appropriate body changes.

These senses can also be thought of as the systems of **perception**, which is concened with how we obtain information from the environment and what we make of it. Learning theorists agree that the forms of perception most involved in learning are **auditory** perception, **visual** perception, **kinesthetic** perception and **tactile** perception. Auditory perception is the mental interpretation of what a person hears. Visual perception is the mental interpretation of what a person sees. Kinesthetic perception is the mental interpretation of the sensation of body movement. Tactile perception is the mental interpretation of what a

---

[2] Barbara B. Brown, *New Mind New Body* (New York, Bantam Books, Inc., 1975), p. 5.

[3] Robert M. Stern and William J. Ray, *Biofeedback and the Control of Internal Bodily Activity* (Homewood, IL, Learning Systems Company, 1975), p. 1.

[4] Barbara B. Brown, *The Biofeedback Syllabus* (Springfield, IL, Charles C Thomas Publisher, 1975), p. vi.

[5] Matthew U. Culligan and Keith Sedlacke, *How to Kill Stress Before It Kills You* (New York, Grossett & Dunlap Publishers, 1976), p. 97.

person experiences through the sense of touch. In this connection, it is common practice among learning theorists to refer to auditory feedback, visual feedback, kinesthetic feedback, and tactile feedback.

BIOFEEDBACK INSTRUMENTATION

We are all aware of the fact that the human body itself is a complicated and complex biofeedback instrument, which alerts us to certain internal activity. However, many students of the subject feel that there is still a need for sensitive instruments to monitor physiological and psychological reactivity.

We are reminded by Stewart Bedford[6] that biofeedback has been around since primitive man looked at his reflections in quiet ponds or streams. He also suggests that biofeedback instruments have been around for a long time with such questions as When was the last time you looked into a mirror? and How long has it been since you weighed yourself? In the discussion here we are thinking of more sophisticated biofeedback instrumentation. Following is a brief discussion of some of the more widely known biofeedback instruments that are used for both research and therapeutic purposes.

Electromyograph (EMG)

Electromyography is the recording of electric phenomena occurring in muscles during contraction. Needle or skin electrodes are used and connected with an oscilloscope so that action potentials may be viewed and recorded (the oscilloscope is an instrument that visually displays an electrical wave on a fluorescent screen). Before the electromyograph was available, guesswork ordinarily had to be used to try to determine the participation of the muscles in movement. When a muscle is completely relaxed or inactive, it has no electric potential; however, when it is engaged in contraction, current appears.

It is believed that EMG training can produce deep muscle relaxation and relieve tension. A person gets the feedback by seeing a dial or hearing a sound from the machine, and he knows immediately the extent to which certain muscles may be relaxed or tensed. A muscle frequently used in EMG training for research and other purposes is the **frontalis** located in the front of the head.

---

[6] Stewart Bedford, *Stress and Tiger Juice* (Chico, CA, Scott Publications, 1980), p. 57.

Another important aspect of EMG is that which is concerned with re-training a person following an injury or disease when there is a need to observe small increments of gain in function of a muscle.

Feedback Thermometers

The obvious purpose of feedback thermometers is to record body temperatures. Ordinarily, a thermistor is attached to the hands or the fingers. This highly sensitive instrument shows very small increments of degrees of temperature change so that the person receives the information with a visual or auditory signal. This kind of feedback instrumentation has been recommended for such purposes as reduction of stress and anxiety and autonomic nervous system relaxation.

Electroencephalograph (EEG)

The purpose of this instrument is to record amplitude and frequency of brain waves, and it has been used in research for many years. It has also been used with success to diagnose certain clinical diseases. In addition, EEG feedback has found use in psychotherapy and in reducing stress as well as pain.

An interesting relatively recent horizon for EEG feedback is how it might be involved in creativity and learning. In fact, some individuals involved in creative activity have indicated that they can emerge from the EEG **theta** state with answers to problems that they previously were unable to solve. The theta waves are ordinarily recorded when a person is in a state of drowsiness or actually falling asleep. It is perhaps for this reason that this condition has been referred to by some as "sleep learning." Since it is a state just before sleep, others refer to it as the twilight period or **twilight learning.**

Barbara Brown contends that EEG could maximize the use of teaching machines. She suggests that the color of the recording screen could be controlled by two basic brain wave patterns: (1) the "alert" EEG associated with high attention levels, and (2) the "non-alert" EEG pattern associated with non-attention. And, similarly physical and mental attitudes more suitable for learning could be learned more readily as well as improvement of their attention span by their own volition.

Galvanic Skin Response (GSR)

There are several different kinds of GSR instruments used to measure changes in electrical resistance of the skin to detect emotional arousal. The instrument reacts in proportion to the amount of perspiration one emits, and the person is informed of the changes in electrical resistance by an auditory or visual signal. One aspect of GSR is concerned with the use of the polygraph or lie detector, which is supposed to record a response that is concerned with lying. GSR feedback is oftentimes recommended for use of relaxation, reducing tension, improvement of ability to sleep, or for emotional control.

In general, the purpose of the biofeedback machinery is to provide accurate and reliable data that will increase one's awareness of how the body is functioning and demonstrate one's influence of his action of his body. Hopefully, this information should be useful in inspiring a person to take an active self-interest in his own well-being. After such information is received, if it has been obtained under the supervision of a qualified person, there may be a given number of sessions arranged for consultation and training. Perhaps the ultimate objective is for the individual to be able to gain control over his own autonomic nervous system.

As popular and well-advertised as biofeedback machinery has become, it is not without its critics. One such authority on mind-body relationships is Doctor Beata Jencks,[7] who feels that many important purposes can be accomplished without instruments by using the body as its own biofeedback instrument. In fact, she identifies over a dozen of these, including the following: (1) diverse muscle relaxation, (2) change of heart rate and body temperature, (3) change of breathing patterns, (4) decrease of stress and anxiety reactions, (5) mental relaxation, (6) autonomic nervous system relaxation, (7) pain and relief for tension headaches, backaches, and other aches and pains, and (8) improved learning ability, including enhancement of concentration and recall. She indicates, however, that certain of the biofeedback instruments, particularly EMG has important application for retraining of patients following disease and injury.

BIOFEEDBACK FOR CHILDREN

An important aspect in developing an understanding of biofeedback with children is that which is concerned with suitable ways to introduce the concept of this phenomenon. In this regard, one excellent introduction to the principle underlying biofeedback is suggested by Stewart Bedford:[8]

---

[7] Beata Jencks, *Your Body, Biofeedback at Its Best* (Chicago, Nelson-Hall, Inc., 1977), p. 17.

[8] Stewart Bedford, *Stress and Tiger Juice* (Chico, CA, 1980, Scott Publications, 1980), p. 58.

Would you like to try a little biofeedback experiment? Get a thermometer. A small weather thermometer will do the best. First, take your hand temperature. Hold the thermometer lightly between your thumb and forefinger. Wait about a minute — or until the liquid in the thermometer stops moving. Then, write down the temperature so you can remember it. Now, do the relaxation exercises previously recommended.

After you have done the relaxation exercises, take your hand temperature again and write it down. Did it go up? If it did, you probably reduced the stress chemicals in your bloodstream. If your hand temperature was close to body temperature to begin with, it probably didn't go up much — you may not have had much stress chemical in your bloodstream. When you raise your hand temperature by relaxing, you are reducing the chemicals in your bloodstream that cause the smooth muscles in the tiny arterials to contract. That reduces the amount of blood flowing through the vessels at skin level so the temperature in your skin goes down.

Step by step, this is the way it works. Somewhere in your mind you decide to tense or relax your muscles. You send messages from the outer part of your brain, your cerebral cortex, to your muscles, telling them what to do. These messages travel down your motor nerves in a way that is like electrical energy going down a wire. If you want to tense your muscles, you zap them with more electrical energy. If you want to relax your muscles, you reduce the amount of electrical energy. When the stress chemicals are reduced, the smooth muscles in your arterials allow the vessels to enlarge. When the vessels enlarge, you have more blood flowing through them and your skin temperature goes up. In this way, you can decide to raise or lower your hand temperature. You can decide to control your stress energy. Remember, though, it will take a lot of practice before you're able to do this quickly.

If you are having a lot of stress, your hand temperature could be less than 70 degrees Fahrenheit (98.6 is normal). If you don't have much stress chemical in your bloodstream, your hand temperature will be just a little below body temperature.

After you have practiced relaxation and have recorded your hand temperature a number of times, you will get good at guessing. You will have incorporated a biofeedback method into your own system.

Biofeedback for children has been used both in the clinical and school settings; however, it has found more prevalent use in the former and it is in this setting where most research has been undertaken. Following are some examples of such research.

Among the prominent researchers in this are two of my former collaborators, John Carter and Harold Russell.[9] They did a study which

---

[9] John L. Carter and Harold Russell, Use of biofeedback relaxation procedures with learning disabled children, in *Stress in Childhood,* ed. James H. Humphrey (New York, AMS Press, Inc., 1984), pp. 277-300.

included 11 treatment combinations and three age ranges with a total of 132 subjects of whom 114 completed the program. Each student received his randomly assigned treatment combination two times per week for six weeks. The four individual treatment components were: (1) EMG biofeedback 20 minutes each time, (2) handwriting practice, (3) prerecorded relaxation audio tapes, and (4) homework with prerecorded audio tapes. They were given a comprehensive battery, including the Slosson Intelligence Test, one week before and one week after treatment. They found that listening to prerecorded relaxation tapes was the best predictor of gains in reading comprehension, and that biofeedback training significantly enhanced the predictability. In fact, the children who received biofeedback and heard the tapes showed significant change in 10 of the 11 measures. The change was maintained or improved over time (10-month follow-up). Children who did not receive the treatments showed improvement on only 1 of 11 variables and the follow-up scores tended to decrease slightly if not significantly. Significant improvements were obtained in verbal IQ, reading, spelling, arithmetic computation, auditory memory, eye-hand coordination and written expression.

Houts[10] administered three weeks of relaxation training followed by weekly thermal biofeedback sessions to an 11-year-old boy who had suffered severely from headaches since he was 6 years old. The boy's headache frequency was greatly reduced. A one-year follow-up revealed that headache frequency remained negligible. Results suggest that child migraine may be amenable to procedures reported to be effective with adult migraine.

Omizo and his associates[11] examined the effects of electromyogram (EMG) biofeedback and relaxation training on memory task performance by hyperactive 9–11-year-old boys. Forty-eight subjects were identified through teachers' ratings on the Conners Behavior Rating Scale — Abbreviated Form and divided into experimental and control groups. Experimental treatment consisted of three 2-phase (biofeedback and relaxation training) EMG sessions. Controls' EMG equipment was inoperative so they did not receive biofeedback or relaxation training. Subjects completed pre- and post-treatment memory tasks — a paired associate word list (the Dolch Basic Memory List) and picture — recall

---

[10] Arthur C. Houts, Relaxation and thermal feedback treatment of child migraine headache: A case study, *American Journal of Clinical Biofeedback* Fall/Winter 5 (1982):154-157.

[11] M.M. Omizo, W.E. Cubberly, S.G. Semands, and S.A. Omizo, The effects of biofeedback and relaxation training on memory tasks among hyperactive boys, *Exceptional Child* March, 33 (1986): 56-64.

tasks (the Peabody Picture Vocabulary Test (PPVT). Results showed that experimental subjects performed better on the paired associate test and achieved better muscle relaxation than controls. Performance on the PPVT did not prove to be significantly different for experimental and control groups when effects of post-EMG recordings and performance on the paired associate word list were controlled for, although univariate F values and multiple analysis of variance procedures revealed significant differences between groups on all variables examined.

Three boys aged 9-11 years meeting multiple criteria of hyperactivity were trained by Raymer and Poppen[12] to emit 10 specific relaxed behaviors by means of behavioral relaxation training (BRT). Dependent measures included a behavioral relaxation scale, frontalis EMG, parent symptom questionnaire, and self-reports. A multiple-probe design across subjects was employed, plus a reversal between recliner and beanbag chair for each subject. BRT was effective in producing high levels of relaxed behaviors and low EMG levels in the office setting, particularly in conjunction with the beanbag chair, with some reduction of hyperactivity scores on the parent questionnaire. Subsequent training in each child's home by his mother was accompanied by further reductions in parent-reporting symptoms and low EMG levels, which were maintained at a one-month follow-up.

Denkowski and Denkowski[13] proposed the question: Is group progressive-relaxation training as effective with hyperactive children as individual EMG biofeedback treatment? This study examined whether group progressive-relaxation training was as effective as individual EMG biofeedback training in facilitating the academic achievement and self-control of 45 hyperactive elementary school children. Academic achievement was assessed with the Gates-MacGinities Reading Tests, and self-control was measured with the Nowicki-Strickland and Teacher Rating Scales. Eight sessions were scheduled at weekly intervals. Progressive relaxation was conducted in groups of 7 or 8 and was induced with a commercial audiocassette program. EMG training augmented frontalis biofeedback with those taped exercises. A placebo group listened to taped children's stories. Multivariate analysis of variance indicated no significant differences among the three contrast groups when

---

[12] R. Raymer and R. Poppen, Behavioral relaxation training with hyperactive children, *Journal of Behavior Therapy and Experimental Psychiatry* December, 16 (1985):309-316.

[13] Kathryn M. Denkowski and George C. Denkowski, Is group progressive relaxation training as effective with hyperactive children as individual EMG biofeedback treatment? *Biofeedback and Self-Regulation* 2 (1984):253.

all dependent variables were considered together. However, univariate F values and discriminant analysis disclosed locus of control to be significantly more internal for the progressive relaxation condition. Also, differences between the two relaxation and placebo groups, though not statistically significant, were all in the expected direction. Although the relative efficacy of group progressive relaxation could not be established conclusively, the data appeared sufficiently positive to warrant further investigation.

Karnes, Oehler and Jones[14] investigated the relationship between biofeedback and tension, as measured by an EMG and Children's Personality Questionnaire (CPQ), in 37 intellectually gifted fourth to seventh graders. Results showed that indirect factors that measure tension on the CPQ were correlated significantly with biofeedback measures. Those subjects who became the most relaxed during biofeedback training appeared to be the least tense on the CPQ. Contrary to these findings, the relaxed-tense factor of the CPQ was correlated significantly and negatively with biofeedback measures, which indicates that the subjects may not have been aware of their own tense state and thus would benefit from biofeedback training.

Another study, by Omizo and Williams[15] examined the effects of biofeedback-induced relaxation training on attention to task, impulsivity, and locus of control among 32 learning disabled children between the ages of 8 and 11 years. Attention to task and impulsivity were measured by the Matching Familiar Figures Test and the locus of control was measured by the Nowicki-Strickland Scale. Participants were randomly assigned to experimental (N = 16) and control (N = 16) groups. The study lasted for eight weeks, with the experimental treatment consisting of three sessions spaced approximately two weeks apart. The treatment included EMG biofeedback training used with relaxation tapes. Univariate F values and discriminant analysis procedures revealed that the attention to task and impulsivity measures proved to be valid discriminators, respectively, beyond the 0.01 and 0.05 levels of significance. Experimental group subjects had a significantly fewer number of errors on the attention to task measure and significantly lower

[14] Frances A. Karnes, Judy J. Oehler, and Gary E. Jones, The relationship between electromyograph level and the Children's Personality Questionnaire as measures of tension in upper elementary gifted students, *Journal of Clinical Psychology* March, 41 (1985):169-172.

[15] Michael M. Omizo and Robert E. Williams, Biofeedback-induced relaxation training as an alternative for the elementary school learning-disabled child, *Biofeedback and Self-Regulation* 7 (1982):139.

impulsivity scores. It was concluded that the biofeedback-induced relaxation training affords promise in assisting learning-disabled children in reaching their educational potentials. It was recommended that future research examine the long-term efficacy and the transfer to school-related tasks of this intervention.

In a final study reported here involving the effect of frontal EMG biofeedback training on the behavior of children with activity-level problems, Hughes, Henry and Hughes[16] employed N = 1 withdrawal designs with three children with such problems. Tutoring sessions occurred daily over a 2.5-month period. Each child was reinforced for decreasing frontalis muscle tension during auditory feedback while working arithmetic problems. Feedback was faded while tension reduction reinforcement was maintained. These procedures were repeated with reinforcement for increasing, rather than decreasing, muscle tension. Frontal EMG level, percent of time on task and motoric activity rate were obtained during sessions. Parent ratings of problem behavior in the home were recorded daily. Biofeedback with reinforcement was effective in both raising and lowering muscle tension. Effects were maintained by reinforcement. Results suggest a direct relationship between tension and activity levels. Academic performance and problem behavior improved significantly with reductions in EMG activity, although individual exceptions to these findings were present. Results lend support to the efficacy of frontal EMG biofeedback training in reducing activity, increasing attention to an academic task, and reducing problem behaviors.

Biofeedback in the school setting has tended to meet with success. For example, Engelhardt[17] developed a program in Spearfish, South Dakota. Under the Elementary and Secondary Education Act, P.L. 89-10, Title III, now Title IV-C, funding was awarded over a three-year period to the Spearfish School District for the implementation of the Awareness and Relaxation Through Biofeedback Program. This act allows funds for innovative approaches to education.

The purpose of this program was to help the participating students and/or teachers acquire muscle-relaxation skills, decrease their general anxiety level and improve their self-concept. Pre- and post-baseline readings were recorded with instrumentation. Forty-two educators

---

[16] Howard Hughes, David Henry, and Anita Hughes, The effect of frontal EMG biofeedback training on the behavior of children with activity-level problems, *Biofeedback and Self-Regulation* 5 (1980):207.

[17] L. Engelhardt, Awareness and relaxation through biofeedback in public schools, *Biofeedback and Self-Regulation*, 3 (1987):195.

completed the relaxation program. All of them reduced their muscle tension, and 95 percent reached the designated criterion level of five microvolts (peak to peak 95-1000 Hz). Pre-baseline the average EMG was 13.5 microvolts, and post-baseline it was 4.64 microvolts. Their hand temperature increased an average of 4.7 degrees Fahrenheit. One hundred and ninety-four students learned relaxation skills using the biofeedback instruments. Their baseline reading was 8.07 and post-program baseline was 3.34 microvolts. They averaged an increase of 6.45 degrees on skin temperature, from 86.36 to 92.81 degrees Fahrenheit. Total instrument practice time per participant was 5 to 15 minutes, two times a week for six weeks. The program has been implemented as curriculum components in a variety of educational areas and grade levels in the Spearfish school system.

It was concluded that muscle-relaxation skills can be acquired as a health practice by both students and teachers as part of their educational curriculum. Teachers first acquired the skills themselves and then implemented the awareness activities, progressive relaxation exercises, passive exercises and biofeedback training with EMG and temperature trainers. Analysis of pre- and post-measurements showed that participants decreased their anxiety level significantly and increased their self-concept scores. Biofeedback instruments demonstrated that students can decrease the frontalis muscle-tension level and/or an increased hand temperature during the routine of the public school classroom. The program was so well received and integrated into the school system that although Doctor Engelhardt's project ended in 1979, it is still in effect at the present time.

One important aspect of this program is the fact that in order to improve the functioning of children, the functioning of adults was improved first. This is consistent with theory regarding the importance of decreasing overreactivity and increasing the functioning of the adult to affect a change in the child.

It has been the concern of some that teachers might not be able to deal effectively with biofeedback procedures. However, in their work, Carter and Russell demonstrated with 650 learning disabled children and 82 teachers in 24 different schools that a packaged kit composed of prerecorded relaxation tapes and a handwriting workbook with instructions could be used effectively by teachers.

At the present time, it is difficult to determine unequivocally what the future of biofeedback may be. Without question, it has influenced our way of thinking with reference to a person being able to possibly control his physiological functions. In view of this, perhaps one of its foremost contributions is that it creates in an individual a feeling of his own responsibility for his personal well-being. It has been suggested that if biofeedback as a research methodology and treatment approach can survive biofeedback as a fad, then it may provide a useful tool that will change our conception of the human body.

BIBLIOGRAPHY

Adamson, C. Creativity in the classroom. Pointer, Spring 1985, 11-15.

Arerickaner, M., and Summerlin, M.L. Group counseling with learning disabled children: Effects of social skills and relaxation training on self-concept and classroom behavior. *J Learn Dis,* June/July 1982, 340-343.

Andre, J.C., and Means, J.R. Rate of imagery in mental practice: An experimental investigation. *J Sport Psychol,* June 1986, 124-128.

Aransky, V.S., and Klarin, M.V. Modern teaching: The strategy of the didactic game in the teaching process. *Int Rev Educ,* March 1987, 312-315.

Ayres, J., and Hopf, T.S. Visualization, systematic desensitization and rational emotive therapy. *Commun Educ,* 36, 236-240.

Balog, L.F. The effects of exercise on muscle tension and subsequent muscle relaxation training. *Res Q Exercise and Sport,* June 1983, 119-125.

Barry, Elizabeth E. "A relaxation therapy program for hyperactive children." *Doctoral dissertation,* Texas A & M University, College Station, Texas, 1982.

Beiser, H.R. On curiosity: A developmental approach. *J Am Acad Child Psychiatry,* September 1984, 517-526.

Blair, M.R., and Vallerand, R.J. Multimodal effects of electromyographic biofeedback: Looking at children's ability to control precompetitive anxiety. *J Sport Psychol,* December 1986.

Bollenback, C. How do you feel on the first day of school? *Learning,* September 1980, 56.

Brandon, Jeffrey E., Eason, Robert Li, and Smith, Theresa L. Behavioral relaxation training and motor performance of learning disabled children. *Adapted Physical Activity Q,* January 1986, 67-79.

Brandon, Jeffrey E., and Poppen, R. A comparison of behavioral, meditation, and placebo control relaxation training procedures. *Health Educ,* October/November 1985, 42-46.

Brockberg, H.F., and Brockberg, K.H. Relaxation is for children too. *Luth Educ,* November/December 1980, 108-114.

Brooks, Wayne W. "Effect of relaxation training on levels of field dependence-independence and reading achievement of elementary school children." *Doctoral dissertation,* Oklahoma State University, Stillwater, Oklahoma, 1985.

Cahoon, P. Meditation magic. *Educ Leadership,* 45, 92-94.

Calderone, M.S. Children: Prime asset, endangered species. *SIECUS Rep,* March 1984, 7-8.

Carter, J.L., and Russell, H.L. Use of EMG biofeedback procedures with learning disabled children in a clinical and educational setting. *J Learn Disabil,* April 1985, 213-216.

Christie, D.J. et al. Using EMG biofeedback to sequel hyperactive children when to relax, *Except Child,* April 1984, 547-548.

Cole, Phyllis L. "The effects of taped relaxation training on physiological events and home and classroom behavior of hyperactive children." *Doctoral dissertation,* Utah State University, Logan Utah, 1981.

Crowley, J.A. Worries of elementary school students. *El Sch Guid and Coun,* December 1981, 98-102.

Cycenas, F. Creative thoughts. *Gifted Child Today,* May/June 1987, 16-21.

Danielson, H.A. The quieting reflex and success imagery. *El Sch and Coun,* December 1984, 152-155.

Day, R.C., and Sadeh, S.N. Effect of Benson's relaxation response on the anxiety levels of Lebanese children under stress. *J Exper Child Psychol,* October 1982, 350-356.

Dickerson, M.G., and Davis, M.D. Developmental approach: A successful way to mainstream the young child. *Childh Educ,* September/October 1981, 8-13.

Duenk, L.G. Games promote more than fun. *Ind Educ,* March 1987, 34-35.

Dunn, Freeman M., and Howell, Robert J. Relaxation training and its relationship to hyperactivity in boys. *J of Clin Psychol,* January 1982, 92-100.

Elkind, D. Piagetian psychology and the practice of child psychiatry. *J Am Acad Child Psychiatry,* September 1982, 435-445.

Fentress, David W. et al. Biofeedback and relaxation-response training in the treatment of pediatric migraine. *Dev Med & Child Neuro,* April 1986, 139-146.

Franks, B.D. Physical activity and stress. *Int J Phys Educ,* April 1984, 9-16.

Galyean, B.C. Guided imagery in the curriculum. *Educ Lead,* March 1983, 54-58.

Garrard, W. Developing children's imagery. *Times Educ Suppl,* May 9, 1986, 3645-3659.

Godin, G., and Shephard. Normative beliefs of school children concerning regular experience. *J Sch Health,* December 1984, 443-445.

Greeson, L.E., and Vane, R.J. Imagery based elaboration as an index of EMR children's creativity and incidental associated learning. *Educ Train Ment Retarded,* September 1986, 174-180.

Harris, P.L. et al. Children's knowledge of emotion. *J Child Psychol and Psychiatry,* July 1981, 247-261.

Horton, J.A. Imagery in our daily lives. *Read Improv,* Spring 1984, 14-17.

Hughes, R. et al. Development of empathic understanding in children. *Child Devel,* March 1981, 122-128.

Humphrey, James H. *Human Stress: Current Selected Research,* Vol. 2. New York, AMS Press, Inc., 1987.

Humphrey, James H. *Human Stress: Current Selected Research,* Vol. 1. New York, AMS Press, Inc., 1986.

Humphrey, James H. *Profiles in Stress.* New York, AMS Press, Inc., 1986.

Humphrey, James H., Editor. *Stress in Childhood.* New York, AMS Press, Inc., 1984.

Humphrey, James H., and Humphrey, Joy N. *Controlling Stress in Children.* Springfield, Illinois, Charles C Thomas Publisher, 1985.

Humphrey, James H., and Humphrey, Joy N. *Reducing Stress in Children Through Creative Relaxation.* Springfield, Illinois, Charles C Thomas, 1981.

Humphrey, James H., and Humphrey, Joy N. *Helping Children Understand About Stress.* Long Branch, New Jersey, Kimbo Educational, 1980.

Humphrey, James H., and Humphrey, Joy N., *Ted Learns About Stress.* Long Branch, New Jersey, Kimbo Educational, 1980.

Jasnow, Mark. "Effects of relaxation training and rational emotive therapy on anxiety reduction in sixth grade children." *Doctoral dissertation,* Hofstra University, Hempstead, New York, 1983.

Karper, W.B. Use of exercise in alleviating emotional disturbance: A review of the literature. *J Sp Educators,* Fall 1981, 61-72.

Knepper, W. et al. Emotional and social problem-solving thinking in gifted and average elementary school children. *J Genet Psychol,* March 1983, 25-30.

Kraft, R.E., and McNeil. Children and Stress: Coping through physical activities. *Phys Educ,* Spring 1985, 72-75.

McKroll, M. Stress management programme for children. *Early Child Dev Car,* March 1986, 191-206.

Margolis, H. Self-induced relaxation: A practical strategy to improve self-concepts, reduce anxiety and prevent behavioral problems. April 1987, 355-358.

Marks, I. The development of normal fear: A review. *J Child Psychol Psychiatry Allied Discip,* September 1987, 67-97.

Martin, A. Encouraging youngsters to discuss their feelings. *Learning 87,* July/August 1987, 80-81.

Martinez, J.G.R. Preventing math anxiety: A prescription. *Acad Ther,* November 1987, 117-125.

Mathews, D.B. Discipline: Can it be improved with relaxation training? *El Sch Guid Coun,* February 1986, 194-200.

Moyer, J. Child development as a base for decision making. *Child Educ,* May/June 1986.

Nardone, Maria J. "A comprehensive group treatment program to teach self-control to impulsive/agressive boys." *Doctoral dissertation,* Fordham University, New York, New York, 1982.

Naylor, A. Teachers' inventory of children's emotional and behavioral development. *Child Today,* November/December 1981, 2-6.

Neumann, P. What do you say to a child in tears? *Instructor,* September 1984, 52-54.

Nold, A.L. A look into the stillness. *Indep Sch,* Spring 1987, 37-40.

Oldfield, D. The effects of the relaxation response on self-concept and acting out behaviors. *El Sch Guid and Coun,* April 1986, 255-260.

Oldfield, D., and Petosa, R. Increasing student "on task" behaviors through relaxation strategies. *El Sch Guid and Coun,* February 1986, 180-186.

Omizo, M.M. Relaxation training and biofeedback with hyperactive elementary school children. *El Sch Guid and Coun,* April 1981, 329-332.

Omizo, M.M. Effects of relaxation and biofeedback training on dimensions of self-concept among hyperactive male children. *Educ Res Q,* Spring 1980, 22-30.

Omizo, M.M., and Michael, W.B. Biofeedback-induced relaxation training and impulsivity, attention to task, and locus of control among hyperactive boys. *J Learn Disab,* August/September 1982, 414-416.

Omizo, M.M., and Williams, R.E. Biofeedback training can calm the hyperactive child. *Acad Ther,* September 1981, 43-46.

Osborn, Evelyn L. Effects of participant modeling and desensitization on childhood warm water phobia. *J Beh Ther & Exp Psychiatry,* June 1986, 117-119.

Pederson, D. Systematic desensitization as a model for dealing with the reticent student. *Comm Educ,* July 1980, 229-233.

Petosa, R., and Oldfield, D. A pilot study of the impact of stress management techniques on the classroom behavior of elementary school children. *J Sch Health,* February 1985, 69-71.

Porter, Sally S., and Omizo, M.M. The effects of group relaxation training/large muscle exercise and parental involvement on attention to task, impulsivity and locus of control among hyperactive boys. *Except Child,* March 1984, 54-64.

Pressure abolishing child (symposium). *Childh Educ,* November/December 1981, 66-87.

Ragan, L., and Hiebert. Kiddie QR (Quieting Reflex): Field testing a relaxation program for young children. *Sch Couns,* March 1987, 273-281.

Richter, Neil C. "Relaxation training with impulsive first grade students." *Doctoral dissertation,* University of South Carolina, Columbia, South Carolina, 1986.

Rider, M.S. et al. The effect of music, imagery and relaxation on adrenal corticosteroids and the re-entrainment of circadian rhythms. *J Music Ther,* Spring 1985, 46-58.

Ritson, R. How to calm down tense kids. Instructor, May 1984, 30-31.

Roberts, N.M. Imagery: A second look, expanding its use in the classroom. *Read Improv,* Spring 1983, 22-27.

Roome, J.R., and Romney, D.M. Reducing anxiety in gifted children by inducing relaxation. *Roeper Rev,* February 1985, 177-179.

Runco, M.A. The generality of creative performance in gifted and nongifted children. *Gifted Child Q,* Summer 1987, 121-125.

Russell, R.K., and Lent, R.W. Cue-controlled relaxation and systematic desensitization versus nonspecific factors in treating test anxiety. *J Counsel Psychol,* January 1982, 100-103.

Saigh, P.A., and Antoun, F.T. Endemic imagery and the desensitization process. *J Sch Psychol,* Summer 1984, 177-183.

Sallade, J.B. Group counseling with children who have migraine headaches. *El Sch Guid and Coun,* October 1980, 87-89.

Schultz, E.W., Teaching coping skills for stress and anxiety. *Teach Except Child,* Fall 1980, 12-15.

Sharpley, C.F., and Rowland, S.E. Palliative vs. direct action stress-reduction procedures as treatment for reading disability. *Br J Educ Psychol,* February 1986, 40-50.

Sigel, J.E. Reflections on action theory and distancing theory. *Hum Dev,* May/April 1984, 188-193.

Sime, W.E. et al. Coping with mathematics anxiety: Stress management and academic performance. *J Coll Stud Pers,* September 1987, 431-437.

Slavenas, R., and Scriven, G.H. (Eds.). Coping with crisis and change. *Early Child Dev Care,* March 1984, 279-397.

Smead, Rosemarie. "A comparison of counselor administered and tape-recorded relaxation training on decreasing target and non-target anxiety in elementary school children." *Doctoral dissertation,* Auburn University, Auburn, Alabama, 1981.

Snyder, Teresa T. "The effects of relaxation training on the behavior of self-contained emotionally handicapped children in the public school setting." *Doctoral dissertation,* North Carolina State University, Raleigh, North Carolina, 1985.

Spillios, James C. Anxiety and learning disabilities. *Sch Psychol Int,* July 1983, 141-152.

Spillios, James C., and Janzen, Henry L. The effect of relaxation therapy on achievement for anxious learning disabled children. *Sch Psychol Int,* April/June 1983, 101-107.

Stanton, H.E. Modification of locus of control using RSI technique in the schools. *Contemp Educ Psychol,* April 1982, 190-194.

Suler, J.R., and Rizziello. Imagery and verbal procession in creativity. *J Creat Behav,* January 1987, 1-6.

Terwogr, M.M. et al. Self-control of emotional reactions by young children. *Psychiatry Allied Discip,* May 1986, 357-366.

The young child at school (symposium). *Educ Leadership,* November 1986, 3-12.

Tomassetti, John T. "An investigation of the effects of EMG biofeedback training and relaxation training on dimensions of attention and learning of hyperactive children." *Doctoral dissertation,* Loyola University, Chicago, Illinois, 1985.

Torrance, E.P. Are children becoming more creative? *J Creat Behav,* September 1986, 1-13.

Treffinger, D.J. Research on creativity. *Gifted Child Q,* Winter 1986, 15-19.

Tyson, R.L. The roots of psychopathology and our theories of development. *J Am Acad Child Psychiatry,* January 1986, 12-22.

Wallace, James I. "Effects of relaxation and physical conditioning programs upon impulsivity in third and fourth grade males." *Doctoral dissertation,* University of Southern California, Los Angeles, California, 1985.

Wardle, F. Getting back to basics of children's play. *Child Care Inf Exch,* September 1987, 27-30.

Weiss, M.R., and Bressan, E.S. Connections-relating instructional theory to children's psychological development. *J Phys Educ Recreat Dance,* November/December, 1985, 34-36.

Wilfley, D., and Kunce, J. Differential physical and psychological effects of exercise. *J Couns Psychol,* July 1986, 337-342.

Williams, D. Maximizing creative potential. *Roeper Rev,* November 1985, 89-92.

Wilson, Barbara J. "Visual exposure and verbal explanation components of a desensitization procedure to reduce children's fear reactions to mass media: a developmental study." *Doctoral dissertation,* University of Wisconsin, Madison, Wisconsin, 1986.

Winn, M. The loss of childhood. *Forecast, Home Econ,* October 1983, 38-46.

Wolfendale, S. The place of parents in child development. *Early Child Dev Care,* February 1983, 85-110.

Yuille, J.C., and Sereda, L. Positive effects of meditation: A limited generalization? *J App Psychol,* June 1980, 333-340.

Zaichkowsky, L.B. et al. Biofeedback-assisted relaxation training in the elementary classroom. *El Sch Guid and Coun,* April 1986, 261-267.

Zenker, E. et al. Improving writing skills through relaxation training. *Acad Ther,* March 1986, 427-432.

Zenker, E., and Frey, D.Z. Relaxation helps less capable students. *J Read,* January 1985, 342-344.

Zigler, E., and Kagan, S.L. Child development and educational practice using what we know. *Natl Soc Stud Educ Yrbk,* January 1982, 80-104.

Zipkin, D. Relaxation techniques for handicapped children: A review of the literature. *J Spec Educ,* Fall 1985, 283-289.

INDEX